Trevor Gray

NATIONAL AND UNIONIST

íReLanɒ

Before the treaty

Blackie

**NATIONALIST
AND UNIONIST**
ireland
before the treaty

© Trevor Gray 1989
First published 1989

British Library Cataloguing in Publication Data

Gray, Trevor
   Nationalist and Unionist: Ireland before the
   Treaty
   1. Ireland. Political events, history
   I. Title
   941.5

ISBN 0-216-92663-7

Blackie and Son Ltd
Bishopbriggs, Glasgow G64 2NZ
7 Leicester Place, London WC2H 7BP

Printed in Great Britain by Scotprint Ltd., Musselburgh, Scotland

Contents

Acknowledgements

The author and publishers have made every effort to trace the ownership of all copyright material and to obtain permission from the holders of the copyright. In a few cases this has proved impossible, and should any question arise as to the use of any selection or any error, it is hoped that the publishers will be informed.

We are grateful to the following sources for permission to reproduce the material indicated.

Northern Ireland Tourist Board page 2

The British Library pages 3, 12, 18

John R. Freeman & Co Ltd page 5

Belfast Library and Society for Promoting Knowledge pages 9, 36, 40 (bottom), 50

The Illustrated London News Picture Library page 13

Library of Congress page 17

National Library of Ireland cover, pages 21, 22 (top right), 43 (top), 53, 59, 60 (bottom), 62, 67, 70, 82 (top), 83

Hulton Picture Company pages 22 (top left), 31 (top), 37 (top), 60 (top), 77, 82 (bottom)

British Library Newspaper Library pages 28, 29, 63 (top)

Public Record Office of Northern Ireland pages 34, 35 (top), 37 (bottom), 38, 39, 40 (top)

Mary Evans Picture Library page 35 (bottom)

National Museum of Ireland pages 43 (bottom), 55, 57, 58

The Commissioners of Public Works in Ireland, at Kilmainham Gaol Museum page 71

The Cork Examiner page 73

Punch pages 74, 81

Municipal Art Gallery, Dublin page 84

Maps and diagram by Kathleen King

To the Teacher

The theme of this book is the development of the Unionist and Nationalist (both constitutional and revolutionary) traditions in the century before the partition of Ireland.

It was felt necessary to trace events from the Norman Invasion until the Act of Union, only in as far as they were relevant to the main theme. For that reason, some aspects of Irish History have been underplayed or ignored. The Irish economy, and especially the development of the linen industry, has not been dealt with, nor have the 18th-century Volunteers and Grattan's Parliament.

It is hoped that these and other omissions will be forgiven; the intention was to keep the story simple, not to mislead the reader.

The wording of the written sources has been tampered with as little as possible.

The questions on the sources are partly comprehension and partly an effort to develop historical skills. They should not be regarded as prescriptive; there is certainly scope for further questions, and for discussion and debate.

It has been left to the teacher to decide whether to demand written or oral responses to the questions.

To the Pupil

Irish History is exciting! It is full of characters who can be seen as heroes or villains, depending on one's point of view. It is full of action, courage, tragedy and disaster.

This book is an attempt to trace the development of the Unionist and Nationalist traditions in Ireland, up to the partition of Ireland in 1921, an understanding of which is essential if the divisions in today's Ireland are to be understood.

It sets before you a variety of historical sources, from which you can obtain evidence about why events took place and why people behaved as they did. You, as a historian, must examine the evidence, ask questions about it, and arrive at sensible conclusions, based on the evidence.

This is how a historian works, and by working with evidence, you should begin to develop some of the skills of the historian, such as the ability to distinguish fact from opinion, the ability to decide about the reliability of source material, and the ability to detect bias in it.

Through the study of this period of Irish History, it is hoped that you will learn tolerance of the opinions of others, that you will come to understand that there is often "right" on both sides, and that you will be encouraged to find out more about Irish History, for this book does not tell the whole story.

Ballymena,   T.J.I.G.
July, 1988

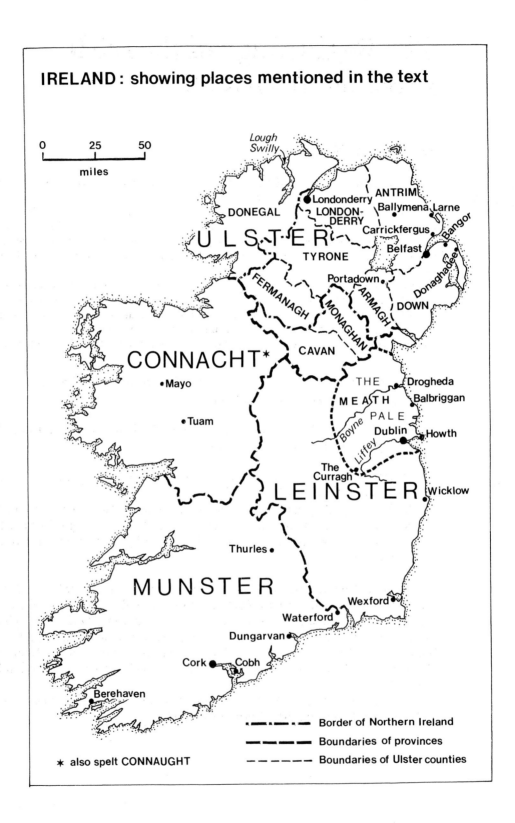

IRELAND: showing places mentioned in the text

0   25   50
miles

Lough Swilly

Londonderry
ANTRIM
DONEGAL
LONDON-DERRY
Ballymena   Larne
U L S T E R
Carrickfergus   Bangor
TYRONE
Belfast
Portadown
Donaghadee
FERMANAGH
ARMAGH
DOWN
MONAGHAN

CONNACHT *
CAVAN

THE   Drogheda
MEATH   Balbriggan
Mayo
PALE
Boyne
Tuam
Dublin   Howth
Liffey

The Curragh
LEINSTER   Wicklow

Thurles

MUNSTER
Wexford
Waterford
Dungarvan
Cork   Cobh
Berehaven

—·—·—·—·— Border of Northern Ireland
————— Boundaries of provinces
------- Boundaries of Ulster counties

* also spelt CONNAUGHT

1 The Beginnings of the Irish Problem 1155-1609

THE NORMANS

"Adrian, bishop, servant of the servants of God, to our well-beloved son in Christ the illustrious king of the English, greeting. . . .

Laudably and profitably does your majesty contemplate spreading the glory of your name on earth and laying up for yourself the reward of eternal happiness in heaven, in that, as becomes a catholic prince, you purpose to enlarge the boundaries of the Church, to proclaim the truths of the Christian religion to a rude and ignorant people. . . .

Whereas then, well-beloved son in Christ, you have expressed to us your desire to enter the island of Ireland in order to subject its people to law and to root out from them the weeds of vice . . ., we therefore . . . do hereby declare our will and pleasure that, with a view to enlarging the boundaries of the Church, . . . you shall enter that island and execute whatsoever may tend to the honour of God and the welfare of that land. . . ."

(From the Papal Bull *Laudabiliter*, by which Pope Adrian IV granted Ireland to King Henry II of England, in 1155.)

With those words, Pope Adrian IV, the only English Pope, gave **Henry II** of England permission to invade Ireland.

1.1 What reasons does the Pope give in Source 1 for granting Henry II permission to invade Ireland?
1.2 Is there anything in Source 1 that would suggest that Henry II might have had other reasons for going to Ireland? What reasons might he have had?
1.3 Is there any reason to suspect that the Pope might have been persuaded to issue this Bull?

At this time, Ireland was ruled by a number of warring chieftains, and it was not until one of them, **Dermot MacMurrough**, King of Leinster, asked Henry II for military aid against his enemies (including Rory O'Connor, King of Connacht and High King of Ireland), that the first Anglo-Normans went to Ireland in 1169. However, these English barons, among them Richard de Clare, Earl of Pembroke (nicknamed "Strongbow"), hoped to seize land for themselves.

When Dermot died in 1171, Strongbow became King of Leinster and, in 1175, Henry II took the title "Lord of Ireland".

SOURCE 2

"This is the agreement which was made at Windsor ... in the year of Our Lord 1175, between Henry, King of England, and Rory, King of Connacht....

The King of England has granted to Rory ..., King of Connacht, as long as he shall faithfully serve him, that he shall be king under him, ready to his service, as his man. And he shall hold his land as fully and as peacefully as he held it before the lord king entered Ireland, rendering him tribute.... And for this agreement the said king of Connacht ... shall not meddle with those lands which the lord king has retained in his lordship and in the lordship of his barons; that is to say, Dublin, ... Meath, ... Wexford, ... the whole of Leinster; and Waterford with its whole territory from Waterford to Dungarvan."

(From the Treaty of Windsor, 1175, between Henry II and Rory O'Connor, High King.)

QUESTIONS

1.4 On what conditions did Henry II allow Rory to keep his lands?
1.5 Do you think it likely that Rory signed this Treaty willingly?
1.6 Does the Treaty of Windsor confirm the ideas you had in answer to Question 1.1?

During the next century, the English overran much of the country, but they did not come in sufficiently large numbers to conquer it completely.

Carrickfergus Castle as it is today. The Castle was begun in the 1180s and was completed in the middle of the 13th century.

Despite building castles like this one in County Antrim, the English never succeeded in controlling more than a small area round Dublin, known as "The Pale". (A "pale" is anything that encloses or fences in, and the modern phrase "to be beyond the pale" means "to be beyond the limit of what is decent", which suggests what the English thought about the rest of Ireland, which was outside their control.)

This was the beginning of what has become known as "**The Irish Question**"—that is, the question of who was to govern Ireland, the Irish or the English.

THE TUDORS

During the 350 years after the Norman Invasion of Ireland, some of the Anglo-Irish families became very powerful in Ireland, and many such as the Butlers, the Burkes, the Savages and the Fitzgeralds adopted Irish customs and the Irish way of life. Indeed, it was after the defeat of a rebellion by one of them—"Silken" Thomas Fitzgerald—that Henry VIII was recognized as King of Ireland by the Irish Parliament, in 1541. (By this time, Henry VIII had quarrelled with the Pope, who was regarded as King of Ireland by many Irishmen.)

SOURCE 3

"Forasmuch as the king our most gracious dread sovereign lord, and his grace's most noble progenitors [i.e. ancestors], kings of England, have been lords of this land of Ireland ... and ... justly and rightfully were, and of right ought to be kings of Ireland.... Wherefore at the ... request of ... the king's loving, faithful and obedient subjects of this his land of Ireland ... be it enacted ... by the authority of this present parliament, that the king's highness, his heirs and successors, kings of England, be always kings of this land of Ireland."

(From "An Act that the King of England, his Heirs and his Successors be Kings of Ireland", 1541.)

QUESTIONS

1.7 Do you think that this change of title might have had anything to do with Henry VIII's recent quarrel with the Pope?

1.8 Do you think Ireland would have been any easier for the English to control now that Henry was King of Ireland? Give a reason for your answer.

Rebellions continued throughout the 16th century. Often the land of the rebels was taken from them, and in parts of Leinster in the 1550s, and Munster in the 1580s, loyal English settlers were given the land (or "planted") in Ireland, in an attempt to make the population easier to control.

A contemporary woodcut showing Irish chieftains submitting to the English Lord Deputy in the 1570s. Notice the difference between the Irish and English fashions.

3

THE PLANTATION OF ULSTER

The most successful of these "plantations" took place in Ulster in 1609, following the defeat of a rebellion there. Rather than accept English domination, Hugh O'Neill, Earl of Tyrone, Hugh O'Donnell, Earl of Tyrconnell and more than ninety of the leading men of Ulster, went into exile in Europe. This "**Flight of the Earls**" left Ulster, which had always been the most difficult part of Ireland for the English to govern, without leaders.

The new King of England, James I (who was also King of Scotland), took the opportunity to carry out "**The Plantation of Ulster**". English and Scottish settlers came to the fertile lands of Ulster in large numbers, bringing with them their own way of life—and their own religion.

RELIGIOUS CONFLICT

Although there had been conflict between the Anglo-Irish and the native Irish, at least they had shared the Catholic faith. But these new English and Scottish settlers were Protestant, and so a religious element entered "**The Irish Question**".

THE THREE PROBLEMS

Therefore, by the 17th century, the three major problems, which were to dominate Irish affairs for the next 300 years, already existed.

(1) English rule.

(2) The ownership of the land.

(3) Religious differences.

2 The Protestants Take Control 1609-1800

17th CENTURY VIOLENCE

The 17th century was a period of great religious bitterness. All over Europe, wars were fought over religious issues, and Ireland was no exception. Violence flared up between Irish Protestants and Irish Roman Catholics at regular intervals. In 1641, the Protestants suffered at the hands of the Catholics; and in 1649, Oliver Cromwell took his revenge.

SOURCE 4

"On a cold November day in 1641 ... a party of some 100 Protestant men, women and children who had been seized from their homes, robbed and stripped of most of their clothes, were herded together onto the bridge [at Portadown]. They were thrown or driven over the parapet into the water below where they were drowned or if they could swim were shot or knocked on the head as they came ashore."

(From *Ireland—A History* by Robert Kee, 1980.)

SOURCE 5

Driuinge Men Women & children by hund:
reds vpon Briges & cafting them into Riuers,
who drowned not were killed with poles &
fhot with mufkets.

G

A 17th century artist's view of events at Portadown in 1641.

SOURCE 6

"[In 1649] Oliver Cromwell was sent to Ireland to deal with the Catholic rebellion. The methods he used to crush the rebels were harsh. When English soldiers captured the garrison of the town of Drogheda they ran wild, killing nearly 3000 people (including 200 women)."

(From *The Irish Question* by Hamish Macdonald, 1985.)

QUESTIONS

2.1 Write a description of the picture in Source 5. Does Source 5 support the account given in Source 4?

2.2 Do you think the artist was a Protestant or a Catholic? Give reasons for your answer.

2.3 Why do you think the picture in Source 5 was drawn?

2.4 Using reference books, try to find out more about Oliver Cromwell.

In 1690, at the **Battle of the Boyne**, King William III of England defeated his Catholic rival, James II. This victory by William of Orange is still commemorated by many Ulster Protestants, because it gave the Protestants the upper hand in Ireland.

THE "PROTESTANT ASCENDANCY"

Gradually the Protestants tightened their control on Ireland. After each period of unrest, more land was confiscated from the Catholics.

SOURCE 7

Table showing the % of Land in Ireland owned by Catholics.
1641—59%
1688—22%
1703—14%
1714— 7%

(Figures taken from *The Course of Irish History* by T. W. Moody and F. X. Martin, 1967.)

As well as this, a series of harsh laws was passed by the Irish Parliament between 1695 and 1727, penalizing or placing restrictions on Irish Catholics.

SOURCE 8

"These 'penal laws' decreed that a Catholic could not hold any office of state, nor stand for Parliament, vote, join the army or navy, practise at the bar, nor ... buy land. A Catholic could not ... even hold land on a lease longer than thirty-one years; nor could he bequeath as he wished what he did hold. On his death his land had to be divided among all his children, unless one of them turned Protestant, in which case he inherited the lot."

(From *Ireland—A History* by Robert Kee, 1980.)

SOURCE 9

"An Act to Prevent the Further Growth of Popery, 1704.

Whereas divers emissaries of the church of Rome, popish priests, and other persons of that persuasion, taking advantage of the weakness and ignorance of some of her majesty's subjects ... do daily endeavour to persuade ... them from the protestant religion ... be it enacted ... that every papist, or person professing the popish religion, shall ... be ... made incapable, to buy ... lands....

[To prove their Protestantism, the following oath had to be sworn] I do solemnly and sincerely, in the presence of God ... declare, that I do believe, that in the sacrament of the Lord's Supper, there is not any transubstantiation of the elements of bread and wine into the body and blood of Christ ... and that the adoration ... of the Virgin Mary, or any other saint, and the sacrifice of the mass, as they are now used in the Church of Rome, are superstitious and idolatrous...."

(From an Act passed by the Irish Parliament in 1704.)

2.5 What is meant by "practise at the bar"?

2.6 What was the point of making Catholic landowners divide their land among their sons (Source 8)?

2.7 What reason is given, in the first few lines of Source 9, for placing these restrictions on the Catholics? Do you think that this was the only reason?

2.8 Do you think the oath in Source 9 would have been an effective way of enforcing these laws? Why do you think so?

2.9 What restrictions mentioned in Source 8 would have made it difficult for Catholics to get these laws changed?

By 1782, Catholics were once again allowed to purchase land and hold leases on land on an equal footing with Protestants. This worried the Protestant minority and it led to outbreaks of violence in the countryside between the Protestant "Peep o' Day Boys" (so-named because they often appeared at dawn to drive their Catholic neighbours off their land), and the Catholic "Defenders".

In 1795, the Peep o' Day Boys formed the Orange Society, later renamed the **Orange Order**. Taking its name from William, Prince of Orange, the Protestant victor at the Battle of the Boyne a century earlier, this society aimed to uphold the Protestant Ascendancy. Members had to swear, "I do solemnly swear that I will, to the utmost of my power, support and defend the King and his heirs as long as he or they support the Protestant ascendancy".

WOLFE TONE, THE UNITED IRISHMEN AND THE 1798 REBELLION

In the 1790s, a new organization came into existence—**The Society of United Irishmen**. One of its founders was a young Protestant Dublin lawyer, **Theobald Wolfe Tone**, who wrote:

"To break the connection with England, the never failing source of all our political evils, and to assert the independence of my country, these were my objects. To unite the whole people of Ireland, to abolish the memory of past dissensions and to substitute the common name of Irishmen in place of the denominations of Protestant, Catholic and Dissenter, these were my means."

(From Wolfe Tone's Journal for 1791.)

The Constitution of the United Irishmen included the words:

"In the present era of reform, when unjust governments are falling in every quarter of Europe ... we think it our duty as Irishmen to ... state what we feel to be our heavy grievance.... We have no national government, we are ruled by Englishmen and the servants of Englishmen, whose object is the interest of another country.... We have agreed to form an association to be called the Society of United Irishmen.... This society is constituted for the purpose of forwarding a ... union of power among Irishmen of every religious persuasion."

(The Constitution of the Societies of United Irishmen, 1797.)

SOURCE 12

Are you straight? ...... I am.
How straight? ...... As a rush.
What have you got in your hand? ...... A green bough.
Where did it first grow? ...... In America.
Where did it bud? ...... In France.
Where are you going to plant it? ...... In the crown of Great Britain.

(From the United Irish catechism.)

SOURCE 13

The badge of the United Irishmen.

UESTIONS

2.10 What were Tone's aims?

2.11 What evidence is there in Source 11 that the United Irishmen were influenced by Wolfe Tone?

2.12 Try to find out what had "first grown in America" (in 1776) and had "budded in France" (in 1789). What does that tell you about the aims of the United Irishmen?

2.13 Explain what you think is meant by the words on the badge.

2.14 Do you think it likely that the United Irishmen would be able to unite "Irishmen of every religious persuasion"? Give reasons for your answer.

The United Irishmen gained support among the Presbyterian Dissenters of Ulster. They too had suffered as a result of the Penal Laws and many favoured complete religious freedom. However, few Catholics joined the United Irishmen. Many of them were satisfied by the easing of the Penal Laws.

The **1798 Rebellion** in which the United Irishmen took part was a failure. Neither it, nor **Robert Emmet's Rebellion** in 1803, achieved its objective of an independent Irish republic. Tone, the first Irish republican, was found guilty of treason, but he committed suicide before he could be executed. Emmet was hanged, drawn and quartered in Dublin.

An artist's impression of the Battle of Antrim, one of the battles in which the United Irishmen took part in 1798. Can you make out the word "Liberty" on their banner?

However, the events of the 1790s were to have a lasting influence on Irish history. The Orange Order, with its determination to defend the privileged position of Irish Protestants, and the violent revolutionary and republican tradition established by Wolfe Tone, both continue to affect Irish politics to the present day.

3 The Act of Union, The Famine and the Beginnings of Nationalism 1801-1850

THE UNION

Following the 1798 Rebellion, the British and Irish Parliaments passed an **Act of Union**. William Pitt, the British Prime Minister saw no way to solve the problem of Ireland but by joining it constitutionally to Britain. (The Union Jack was altered to include the red Cross of Saint Patrick.)

"... The said kingdom of Great Britain and Ireland shall, upon the first day of January ... 1801 ... and for ever, be united into one kingdom by the name of 'The United Kingdom of Great Britain and Ireland'....

That the said united kingdom be represented in one and the same parliament, to be styled 'The Parliament of the United Kingdom of Great Britain and Ireland'.... [32 Irish bishops and lords were to sit in the House of Lords] and one hundred commoners ... be the number to sit and vote on the part of Ireland in the House of Commons of the Parliament of the United Kingdom."

(From The Act of Union, 1800.)

QUESTIONS

3.1 What ceased to exist as a result of this Act?

3.2 How were the Irish people to be represented in Parliament after 1801?

3.3 In what way did this Act bring about the opposite of what Tone had been fighting for?

Most of the Penal Laws had been repealed in the 1780s and 1790s, and the greatest restriction on Roman Catholics was removed by the **Catholic Emancipation Act** (1829), which allowed them to sit in Parliament.

OPPOSITION TO THE UNION

The Catholic majority in Ireland was only a minority in the United Kingdom, and many felt that, although they now had greater freedom, they would have no real political power until a parliament was re-established in Ireland.

DANIEL O'CONNELL AND THE REPEAL ASSOCIATION

In 1840, **Daniel O'Connell**, who had led the struggle for Catholic Emancipation, set up **The Repeal Association**, which campaigned for the repeal of the Act of Union. He hoped that it could be achieved peacefully, and he still swore loyalty to the Crown. Although it failed to achieve its objective, and was dissolved after O'Connell's death in 1847, the desire for repeal lived on and was resurrected in the 1870s in the form of Home Rule (see later).

"I would not ... fling British connection to the winds. I desire to retain it.... What, then, do I propose? That there should be that friendly connection between the two countries which existed before the Union."

(From a speech by Daniel O'Connell to the House of Commons in 1834.)

[The campaign to bring about the repeal of the union] "... must be constitutional in all its intentions.... It must be free from any violence, any breach of the peace or destruction of property."

(From a letter written by Daniel O'Connell to the Repeal Association in 1843.)

THE YOUNG IRELANDERS
In 1846, a group of young men, including Thomas Davis and John Mitchel, left the Repeal Association, rather than support a motion which ruled out the use of force under any circumstances.

Mitchel founded his own newspaper, *The United Irishman*, in which he wrote:

"Let the man amongst you, who has no gun, sell his garment and buy one."

"The Irish people should fight to set up a republic completely cut off from Britain."

"Speeches or resolutions ... never will ... do one bit of good unless we all have arms and are ready to turn out."

(Three extracts written by John Mitchel in his newspaper *The United Irishman*.)

QUESTIONS

3.4 Read Sources 15, 16 and 17 carefully. Do you think either O'Connell or Mitchel looked back to the tradition established by Tone and Emmet?
3.5 Which of the two policies do you think was likely to have the more success? Give reasons for your answer.

In 1848, the **Young Irelanders** organized an uprising, but it was easily crushed and several of the leaders were transported to Tasmania. The Young Ireland movement disintegrated, but it had kept alive the violent republican tradition of Wolfe Tone and Robert Emmet, and one of those who had taken part in the 1848 uprising, James Stephens, was to set up another violent republican organization, the Irish Republican Brotherhood, in 1858 (see later).

(1848 had also seen the appearance, for the first time, of the green, white and orange tricolour, which was to become the flag of the Irish Republic. The colours symbolize the joining together of the older Ireland [green] with the newer Ireland [orange].)

THE FAMINE
The population of Ireland rose from 5.2 million in 1801 to 8.2 million in 1841. The majority of the Irish people depended on farming for a living, and, as the population increased, there was scarcely enough land to feed everyone.

Although there were many good landlords, who did their best for their tenants, much of the land was in the hands of "absentee" landlords, who preferred to live in England and who took little interest in their tenants. The

11

Irish peasants themselves often seemed uninterested in improving their lot. Many insisted on subdividing their land among their sons, despite the difficulties that created.

In 1841, 45% of Irish farms were of five acres or less, and only 18% were larger than fifteen acres. On such small farms, it was often difficult to grow sufficient crops to feed the family and to pay the rent. Tenants were frequently evicted for the non-payment of rent.

SOURCE 18

"It was the most appalling sight I ever witnessed: women, young and old, running wildly to and fro with small portions of their property to save it from the wreck—the screaming of the children, and the wild wailing of the mothers driven from home and shelter.... In the first instance the roof and portions of the walls only were thrown down. But ... the next day the bailiffs were despatched with orders to pull down all the walls and root up the foundations in order to prevent the poor people from daring to take shelter amid the ruins."

(From the *Freeman's Journal*, a newspaper of the 1840s.)

SOURCE 19

A contemporary artist's impression of an eviction scene in Ireland in the 1840s.

QUESTIONS

3.6 What words in Source 18 suggest that the writer was biased in favour of the tenants, rather than the landlords?

3.7 In what ways does Source 19 support the description in Source 18?

3.8 Describe the feelings of an evicted family. Why might they feel sad, frightened, worried, angry? What other feelings might they have had?

Any corn that the farmers grew had to be sold in a desperate attempt to pay their rents, and so the majority of the Irish peasants depended on the potato for survival.

In 1845, disaster struck. A disease which caused the potatoes to rot, either in the ground or shortly after they had been harvested, destroyed three-quarters of the crop; in 1846 the crop was a total failure. The following year the crop was good but small, because the farmers had few potatoes for seed. The crop of 1848 was again a total failure. The people had to rely on private charity or on government help.

The government did set up public work schemes to provide employment which would enable the hungry to buy food and in 1847 it set up soup kitchens to feed the people directly, but to many Irishmen it seemed that it had been too little, too late. During the Famine years, perhaps one million people had died of starvation and disease, and more than a million others emigrated, mostly to America.

SOURCE 20

"Hungry, verminous, fever-ridden, they were herded together on cargo ships hastily adapted to carry this human freight; and they were for the most part too ignorant and too apathetic to attempt the most elementary precautions against infection. Inevitably the rate of mortality was high—of emigrants sailing from Liverpool to Canada in 1847, one in fourteen died at sea, of those sailing from Cork, one in nine; and the memory of the 'coffin ships' is firmly entrenched in the folk-tradition of the famine."

(From *The Making of Modern Ireland* by J. C. Beckett, 1966.)

SOURCE 21

Emigrants leaving Cork for Liverpool on their way to America. (From "Illustrated London News", 10 May, 1851).

 UESTIONS

3.9 Why do you think so many people died on the journey to America?

3.10 Beckett wrote Source 20 over a hundred years after the Famine. Where do you think he got his information?

3.11 Is Beckett's account likely to be more reliable or less reliable than an account written at the time? Explain your answer.

3.12 Sources 19 and 21 are both primary sources. Is there any reason to question their reliability?

The suffering of the Famine years was due to a great number of factors—the rise in the population, economic conditions, lack of understanding of the problem and even perhaps the Irish peasants themselves. But many Irishmen blamed the landlords, and others, like Wolfe Tone half a century earlier, blamed "the connection with England, the never failing source of all our political evils".

"A people, whose land and lives are . . . in the keeping and custody of others instead of their own, are not in a position of common safety. The Irish Famine of '46 is example and proof. The corn crops were sufficient to feed the island. But the landlords would have their rents in spite of the famine, and in defiance of fever. They took the whole harvest and left hunger to those who raised it. Had the people of Ireland been the landlords of Ireland, not a single human creature would have died of hunger."

(James Fintan Lalor, a Young Irelander, in a letter to the journal *The Irish Felon*, June 1848.)

QUESTIONS

3.13 On whom does Fintan Lalor blame the Famine?
3.14 Is there any reason to think that his opinion is biased?
3.15 How do you think he would have remedied the situation?
3.16 Explain in your own words the phrase "in defiance of fever", and the last sentence, beginning "Had the people of Ireland. . . .".

On both sides of the Atlantic, societies, which hoped to break Ireland's connection with Britain, were formed.

4 Nationalism Develops: Republic or Home Rule? 1850-1912

VIOLENT NATIONALISM: THE FENIANS

James Stephens, who had taken part in the 1848 Rising, fled from Ireland shortly afterwards, and during his travels he met John O'Mahony in Paris. O'Mahony eventually went to America, and on St. Patrick's Day 1858, he founded a republican organization, which he called **The Fenian Brotherhood of America**. (The name "Fenian" came from "Fianna", the military force led by Finn MacCool, heroic warrior of Irish legend.)

At the same time, Stephens founded the **Irish Republican Brotherhood (I.R.B.)** in Ireland. Although they were separate organizations, the entire republican movement became popularly known as "The Fenians". The main function of the American organization was to supply the I.R.B. with arms, volunteers and money.

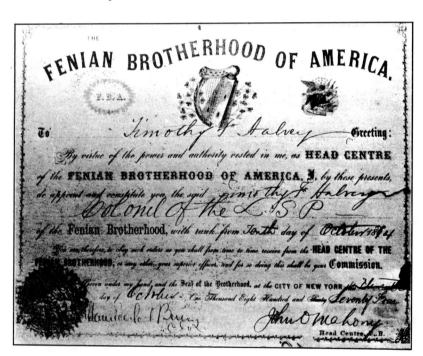

Fenian Membership
Card, signed by John
O'Mahony and dated
1874.

"I, A.B., in the presence of Almighty God, do solemnly swear allegiance to the Irish Republic, now virtually established, and that I will do my utmost, at every risk, while life lasts, to defend its independence and integrity; and finally that I will yield implicit obedience in all things not contrary to the laws of God, to the commands of my superior officers. So help me God."

(One version of the Oath taken by members of The Fenian Brotherhood.)

4.1 Read Source 24 and explain what the aims of the Fenians were.

4.2 What do you think is meant by the phrase "now virtually established"? Was it true, and if not, why do you think the phrase was used?

4.3 What evidence is there from:
(a) the name "Fenians",
(b) the Membership Card,
(c) the Oath,
to suggest that the Fenians were prepared to use violence to achieve their aims?

4.4 Why do you think the Fenians had support in America?

4.5 In the previous sixty years, what other attempts had been made to achieve similar aims?

The Fenians never attracted widespread support in Ireland. Indeed two important groups in Ireland opposed them.
One group was made up of the peaceful nationalist politicians and the other was the Catholic Church. Although some priests supported the Fenians, Cardinal Cullen and most of the Bishops disapproved, and it was declared to be a serious sin to be a Fenian.

SOURCE 25

"We saw clearly that the people should be taught to distinguish between the priest as a minister of religion and the priest as a politician, before they could be got to advance one step on the road to independence. The people for whom God created it, must get this island into their own hands. If they do not, the fruitful land will become a grazing farm for the foreigners' cattle and the remnant of our race, wanderers and outcasts all over the world, if English rule in Ireland be not struck down. Our only hope is in revolution. But most of the bishops and many of the clergy are opposed to revolution.... We have over and over declared it was our wish that the people should respect and be guided by their clergy in spiritual matters. But when priests turn altars into a platform; when it is pronounced a 'mortal sin' to read *The Irish People*, a 'mortal sin' even to wish that Ireland should be free; when priests actually call upon the people to turn informers, and openly threaten to set the police upon the track of men who are labouring in the cause for which our Fathers so often bled; ... — when in a word, bishops and priests are doing the work of the enemy, we believe it is our duty to tell the Irish people that bishops and priests may be bad politicians and worse Irishmen."

(An extract from the Fenian newspaper *The Irish People*, 16 September 1865, First published in 1863, it was suppressed by the government in 1865.)

4.6 What does the writer of Source 25 say will happen if Ireland fails to obtain independence?

4.7 Explain the meaning of the phrase "the people should respect and be guided by their clergy in spiritual matters".

4.8 According to the writer, what steps had the Catholic Church taken in an effort to damage the Fenian movement?

4.9 Why does the writer say that "bishops and priests are doing the work of the enemy"?

4.10 Why do you think the Church was so opposed to the Fenians?

THE 1867 RISING

By 1865, Stephens had decided to stage an armed rebellion. However, information leaked out and many leading Fenians were arrested and sentenced to long terms of imprisonment in British jails.

An attempt to raid Chester Castle, in England, for arms in February 1867 was foiled and when the Rising took place in Ireland in March, it was crushed within 24 hours. For its part in dealing with the Rising, the Irish Constabulary was granted the prefix "Royal".

In England in September, the rescue of two Fenian prisoners, Thomas Kelly and Timothy Deasy, in Manchester, resulted in the death of a police sergeant. Three Fenians, Larkin, Allen and O'Brien were executed for the murder. Although they were present at the time, it is not certain that any of them fired the fatal shot. They became known as "**The Manchester Martyrs**".

SOURCE 26

A poster published in New York, commemorating the execution of Larkin, Allen and O'Brien in November 1867.

 UESTIONS

4.11 What group do you think was responsible for producing this poster?

4.12 Explain the meaning of the phrase "Ireland's Latest Martyrs".

4.13 Study the poster carefully. You might like to discuss the meaning of the different images used by the artist.

Three months after the Manchester incident, an attempt was made to rescue another Fenian, Richard O'Sullivan Burke, from Clerkenwell Prison in London. A barrel of explosives placed against the outside wall of the prison killed twelve people and injured fifty others. A known Fenian, Michael Barrett, who, it was claimed, had been in Glasgow at the time, was charged, found guilty and executed in May 1868.

An artist's impression of the Clerkenwell explosion, published in a London magazine, shortly after the incident.

Although the events of 1867 brought Irish independence no closer, and the Fenians were denounced by Pope Pius IX, the Fenians were to become martyrs in the eyes of some Irishmen. The Fenian movement declined after 1867, but when it was revived at the beginning of the next century, one leading member was to recall the Fenians of 1867; in 1915, Patrick Pearse was to say: "They have left us our Fenian dead, and while Ireland holds their graves, Ireland unfree shall never be at peace".

GLADSTONE AND IRELAND

The Fenian Rising of 1867 had a great effect on at least one English politician. **William Ewart Gladstone**, the leader of the Liberal Party, fought the 1868 General Election under the slogan "Justice for Ireland", and when the Liberals won the election, Gladstone announced, "**My mission is to pacify Ireland**". He hoped to deal with the unrest in Ireland by removing what he saw as the causes.

First he tackled religion. Only about 12% of the Irish population belonged to the Church of Ireland and yet it was the "Established" or State Church, to which the whole population contributed. In 1869, under Gladstone's guidance, Parliament "**disestablished**" the Church of Ireland; it became independent of the state and was supported financially only by its own members, while its property, except for churches actually in use, was confiscated, and the proceeds were used for charitable purposes. In fact, the privileged position of the Church of Ireland was destroyed and all religious denominations were placed on an equal footing.

Secondly Gladstone turned to the land problem. In an effort to protect tenants from eviction, the **1870 Land Act** stated that tenants who were evicted unjustly were entitled to receive compensation. Although the Act was largely ineffective because it did not prevent landlords from evicting tenants for the non-payment of rent, it did set an example of concern for tenants, which later governments, both Liberal and Conservative, were to copy.

Gladstone had attempted to deal with the problems of religion and land, but the basic problem remained; the majority of Irishmen wanted Ireland to have greater control over its own affairs.

CONSTITUTIONAL NATIONALISM: HOME RULE

Isaac Butt, a Protestant lawyer and Member of Parliament, believed that the cause of the discontent and violence in Ireland was the Act of Union. As long as laws for Ireland were made at Westminster, he felt that the country would remain disturbed. Like O'Connell, he wanted to find a peaceful solution, and one that would not break the connection between Great Britain and Ireland, for he knew that most Protestants supported the Union.

In 1870 Butt formed the Home Government Association, which put forward a policy that he hoped would satisfy both the supporters and the opponents of the Union. That policy became known as "Home Rule", and his association was renamed the **Home Rule League** in **1873**, when a conference, which was attended by 900 supporters of Home Rule, including 28 Irish M.P.s, was held in Dublin.

SOURCE 27

"(1) ... We declare our conviction that it is essentially necessary to the peace and prosperity of Ireland that the right of domestic legislation on all Irish affairs should be restored to our country.

(2) ... We declare that the time in our opinion has come when a combined and energetic effort should be made to obtain the restoration of that right.

(3) ... We claim the privilege of managing our own affairs by a parliament assembled in Ireland....

(4) ... The Irish parliament [should have] the right of legislating for ... all matters relating to the internal affairs of Ireland, while leaving to the imperial parliament the power of dealing with all questions affecting ... the relations of the empire with foreign states, and all matters appertaining to [i.e. dealing with] the defence ... of the empire.

(5) Such an arrangement does not involve any change in the existing constitution of the imperial parliament....

(6) ... There should be in Ireland an administration [i.e. government] for Irish affairs, controlled ... by the Irish parliament....

(7) In the opinion of this conference, ... [an] arrangement based on these principles would consolidate the strength ... of the empire....

(8) ... We are willing that there should be ... the amplest guarantees ... that no legislation shall be adopted to establish any religious ascendancy in Ireland....

(9) This conference cannot separate without calling on the Irish constituencies at the next general election to return men … devoted to the great cause which this conference has been called to promote….

(10) In order to carry these objects into practical effect, an association be now formed, to be called 'The Irish Home Rule League', of which … the only object shall be to obtain for Ireland by peaceable and constitutional means, the self-government claimed in those resolutions."

(Extracts from "Proceedings of the Home Rule Conference held in the Rotunda, Dublin, 18–21 November 1873".)

4.14 Compare Source 27 with Source 24. In what ways were the aims of the Home Rule League and the Fenians (a) similar? and (b) different?

4.15 Read Resolutions (3) and (4) carefully. Explain in your own words exactly what the Home Rule League was demanding. Would you describe their aims as moderate, or extreme? Give reasons for your answer.

4.16 In what ways might the demands of the Home Rule League have satisfied both those who supported the Union and those who opposed it?

4.17 Do any of the Resolutions say anything which might have eased the fears of those who supported the Union? Explain your answer.

Since the Union, Irish M.P.s had belonged to either the Liberal Party (formerly the Whigs) or the Conservative Party (formerly the Tories). However in 1874, Home Rule League candidates won 59 seats at Westminster—over half the Irish Members of Parliament. This was the first step towards the creation of a separate **Irish Parliamentary Party** at Westminster (often referred to as the **Irish Nationalist Party**).

PARNELL

The Home Rule Party made little progress, however. What could 59 M.P.s do in a Parliament of over 650? Joseph Biggar, M.P. for Cavan, had an answer. If they could not achieve anything for Ireland, they could at least make their presence felt. He and several other Home Rule M.P.s, including the young M.P. for Meath, **Charles Stewart Parnell**, began a policy of "obstruction", speaking for hours in debates, making sure that Parliament could get little business done.

This policy proved popular in Ireland, and in 1880, 61 Home Rulers were elected. They elected Parnell as their leader, Butt having died in 1879.

"No man has the right to fix the boundary to the march of a nation. No man has the right to say to his country, 'Thus far shalt thou go and no further', and we have never attempted to fix the *ne plus ultra* [i.e. limit] to the progress of Ireland's nationhood and we never shall. But … we must each one of us resolve in our own hearts that we shall at all times do everything that within us lies to obtain for Ireland the fullest measure of her rights."

(From a speech by Parnell at Cork in January 1885.)

4.18 In what ways does this speech suggest that Parnell may have seen Home Rule merely as a first step towards total independence?

Parnell realized that most Irishmen were more interested in land than they were in Home Rule, and so, at a time of agricultural depression and high rents, Parnell became President of the newly formed **Land League** in 1879. The Land League aimed to help tenants to become the owners of their own land, and Parnell hoped that his support for the Land League would in turn gain support for Home Rule.

Both the Liberals (in 1881) and the Conservatives (in 1885) passed Land Acts, which fixed fair rents and gave government grants to help tenants to buy their land, but Parnell remained more interested in Home Rule.

THE FIRST HOME RULE BILL 1886

The 1885 General Election results created an interesting situation. The Liberals won 335 seats, the Conservatives 249 and the Irish Nationalists 86. Parnell's supporters held the balance of power and when Gladstone announced that he now believed that Home Rule was the solution to Ireland's problems, Parnell and the Nationalists promised him their support. And so Gladstone became Prime Minister again.

In 1886, Gladstone introduced the **First Home Rule Bill** in the House of Commons. It proposed setting up in Dublin an Irish Parliament, which would have control over domestic affairs.

Gladstone introducing the First Home Rule Bill into Parliament in 1886.

However, 93 Liberals, led by Joseph Chamberlain, voted with the Conservatives against the Bill and it was defeated in the House of Commons by 343 votes to 313. (Chamberlain and his supporters became known as Liberal Unionists—i.e. Liberals who supported the Union.)

In the General Election which followed, the Conservatives were returned to power.

Four years later, Parnell's political career came to an end when he was forced to resign as leader of his party, following his disgrace in divorce proceedings over his affair with Katharine O'Shea, the wife of a friend.

Mrs Kitty O'Shea.

Charles Stewart Parnell.

SOURCE 29

> Dec: 15th
>
> My own darling Queenie
> Nothing in the world is worth the risk of any harm or injury to you. How could I ever live without my own Katie, and if you are in danger my darling I will go to you at once. Dearest Wifie your letter has frightened me more than I can tell you. Do write my darling and tell me

An extract from one of their love letters.

SOURCE 30

"Parnellism is a simple love of adultery and all those who profess Parnellism profess to love and admire adultery. They are an adulterous set, their leaders are open and avowed adulterers, and therefore I say to you, as parish priest, beware of these Parnellites when they enter your house, you that have wives and daughters, for they will do all they can to commit these adulteries, for their cause is not patriotism—it is adultery."

(From a sermon delivered in the early 1890s in a church near Parnell's home in County Wicklow. Quoted in *Ireland—A History* by Robert Kee, published in 1980.)

4.19 In what ways could Source 30 be described as both reliable and unreliable historical evidence?

4.20 Why do you think Parnell's personal life had such an effect on his political career? Would such behaviour have a similar effect today?

Following the divorce, Parnell married Mrs. O'Shea, in June 1891, but in October of the same year, he died of rheumatic fever, at the age of 45.

THE SECOND HOME RULE BILL 1893

Shortly after the Liberals returned to power in 1892, Gladstone introduced a **Second Home Rule Bill**. This time it was passed by the House of Commons, but was defeated in the House of Lords, which had a Conservative majority.

In 1895, the Conservatives won the General Election, and during the next ten years they attempted to "kill Home Rule with kindness", by introducing further Land Acts, which increased the government grants available to tenants wishing to buy their own land.

4.21 What do you think was meant by "kill Home Rule with kindness"?

4.22 From the knowledge you have gained about Irish history, do you think such a policy was likely to succeed?

THE NATIONALIST PARTY SPLIT

Following Parnell's disgrace, the Irish Nationalist Party had split into Parnellites and Anti-Parnellites. It was only reunited in 1900, under the leadership of John Redmond.

With the Conservatives being opposed to Home Rule, and the Irish Nationalist Party split, no further progress was made towards Home Rule until the Liberals returned to power at the end of 1905.

THE GAELIC REVIVAL

Although Irish Nationalism made little political progress during the 1880s and 1890s, there was a revival of interest in the Irish language and in Irish culture, which made many Irishmen more aware of the differences between British and Irish traditions. In the long run, this strengthened Irish Nationalist feeling.

In 1884 the **Gaelic Athletic Association** was set up "for the preservation and cultivation of our national pastimes", and it soon revived traditional Irish games such as Gaelic football and hurling.

The **Gaelic League**, founded in 1893 by Douglas Hyde and Eoin MacNeill, aimed to restore and preserve the Irish language and to encourage Gaelic literature.

(It is interesting to note how many Protestants have played a part in Irish Nationalism; Tone, Mitchel, Butt, Parnell and Hyde were all Protestants, and they were not the only ones.)

SOURCE 31

"I should like to call attention to the illogical position of men who drop their own language to speak English, of men who translate their euphonious [i.e. pleasant sounding] Irish names into English..., of men who read English books and know nothing about Gaelic literature, nevertheless protesting ... that they hate the country which at every hand's turn they rush to imitate."

(From a lecture by Douglas Hyde entitled *The Necessity for De-Anglicizing Ireland*, 1894.)

SOURCE 32

"An Claidheamh Soluis", the paper of the Gaelic League, first published in 1899.

UESTIONS

4.23 What point is Hyde trying to make in Source 31?

4.24 "An Claidheamh Soluis" means "Sword of Light". Can you suggest any reasons why that title was chosen for the paper of the Gaelic League?

4.25 What do you notice about the advertisements? Can you suggest any reasons for this?

SINN FÉIN AND THE REVIVAL OF THE I.R.B.

Irish Nationalism enjoyed a revival in the early years of the 20th century. Redmond reunited the Irish Nationalist Party at Westminster, and two other developments were to play a part.

One was the setting up of **Sinn Féin** ("Ourselves") by Arthur Griffith in 1904. Its policy was to "boycott" all things British and to set up a parliament in Ireland, to which all Irishmen could give allegiance. The British-based government would then collapse, Griffith believed.

The other development was the revival of the **Irish Republican Brotherhood**, which had almost disappeared at the end of the 19th century. In the early years of the 20th century, young men such as Bulmer Hobson and Seán MacDermott joined the I.R.B. in Belfast, while in Dublin, an old republican, Thomas Clarke, recruited young enthusiastic men into the movement.

Both Sinn Féin and the reactivated I.R.B. were to play important parts in the events of the next twenty years.

5

The Development of Unionism 1801-1912

PROTESTANTS AND THE UNION

Irish Protestants had not at first supported the idea of Union between Great Britain and Ireland. William Pitt, the Prime Minister, had found it necessary to use all his political influence to persuade the Irish Parliament, which was controlled by the Irish Protestants, to vote itself out of existence. (It was claimed that Pitt's "bribery" included 28 Life Peerages, 7 Earldoms, 7 Viscountcies and 3 Marquisates.)

However, the Irish Protestants soon came to see the Union as the surest guarantee of their rights and privileges, for, although they were in a minority in Ireland, there was a Protestant majority when the United Kingdom was considered as a whole.

Protestant support for the Union became even stronger in 1829, when as a result of Catholic Emancipation, Catholics were permitted to sit in Parliament.

"The Protestants of Ireland may rely upon it that their existence and the possession of their properties depend upon the maintenance of the Union.... Let the question of Repeal or no Repeal be a question of Protestant and Catholic."

(From a letter written in 1832 by the Duke of Wellington, leader of the Conservative Party to Lord Roden, Grand Master of the Orange Order.)

Q UESTIONS

5.1 What was meant by "Repeal"?
5.2 Why should Wellington have believed that the Protestants' "existence and the possession of their properties" depended on the continuation of the Union?
5.3 At a time when there was a campaign for the repeal of the Act of Union, what effect would this feeling among Irish Protestants have had on the political and religious atmosphere in Ireland?

The Orange Order, which had been set up to maintain the Protestant Ascendancy, and of which Lord Roden was Grand Master, was seen by many as the surest guarantee of Protestant supremacy. It opposed Catholic Emancipation and Repeal, and its annual celebration of the victory of William of Orange at the Battle of the Boyne in 1690, held each 12 July, often led to sectarian rioting in the 1830s and 1840s. Perhaps the most serious incident took place at Dolly's Brae in County Down in 1849, when Catholics confronted Orangemen returning from a rally at Tullymore, on Lord Roden's estate. Thirty Catholics were killed.

After the dissolution of the Repeal Association, following O'Connell's death in 1847, the threat to the Union seemed to be less serious, and it was only after the formation of the Home Rule League in 1873 that support for the Union became a serious political issue again.

THE UNIONISTS AND THE FIRST HOME RULE BILL 1886

However, prior to 1885, the opponents of the Nationalist movement in Ireland were politically divided, but the growing strength of Parnell's party in Parliament forced them to forget their old party differences, in order to fight the Home Rule candidates in the General Election of November 1885.

In May 1885, the **Irish Loyal and Patriotic Union (I.L.P.U.)** was formed to organize resistance to Home Rule in the three southern provinces. However, only two anti-Home Rule candidates were elected in southern constituencies in November 1885.

Irish "**Unionists**" (as supporters of the Union were called) made up 25% of the population of Ireland. Most Unionists were Protestant and most were descended from the English and Scottish settlers who had come to Ireland in the 17th century. Most lived in the north-east corner of Ireland—part of Ulster—which was much more prosperous than the rest of Ireland, largely thanks to the linen and shipbuilding industries.

5.4 From the above paragraph, pick out three reasons why the Unionists were opposed to Home Rule.

The Unionists had the support of the Conservative Party, which believed that Home Rule was a threat to the unity of the British Empire, and in the 1885 Election, 16 seats in Ulster had been won by Conservatives. However the remaining 17 were won by Nationalists.

In the face of this Nationalist success, the **Ulster Loyalist Anti-Repeal Union** was set up in Belfast in 1886, and later that month the opponents of Home Rule formed the **Irish Unionist Party** in the House of Commons. Col. Edward Saunderson, M.P. for Cavan since 1865, became leader of the party. He had joined the Orange Order in 1882 and he warned that it might be necessary to use physical force to resist Home Rule.

The Ulster Loyalist Anti-Repeal Union organized meetings to oppose Home Rule and there were soon 20 local associations. **Lord Randolph Churchill** (the father of the perhaps more famous Sir Winston), a leading Conservative, was invited to Belfast in February, when he promised support from England and he uttered the ominous words, "**Ulster will fight and Ulster will be right**".

SOURCE 34

"I decided some time ago that if [Gladstone] went for Home Rule, the Orange Card would be the one to play. Please God it may turn out to be the ace of trumps and not the two."

(Lord Randolph Churchill, in a letter to a friend, February 1886.)

SOURCE 35

"Immediately the Orange Order became highly respectable and exceedingly powerful, for people of every class swelled its ranks—country gentlemen, Protestant clergymen, businessmen, tradesmen, labourers, farmers. They flaunted their [Orange] sashes as tokens of loyalty, their drums thundered defiance over the countryside, they vowed to preserve the Union and they chanted Lord Randolph Churchill's slogan 'Ulster will fight and Ulster will be right'."

(From an article by David Hammond in *Two Centuries of Irish History*, published in 1966.)

QUESTIONS

5.5 What do you think is meant by "the Orange Card", in Source 34?

5.6 What evidence is there that Edward Saunderson also believed that "the Orange Card" was "the one to play"?

5.7 Does Source 35 *prove* that the Orange Card had turned out to be " the ace of trumps"?

In the midst of all this Unionist activity, Gladstone introduced the **First Home Rule Bill** into the House of Commons in April 1886.

SOURCE 36

"… there should be reasonable safeguards for the Protestant minority, especially in the province of Ulster. But, sir, I cannot allow it to be said that a Protestant minority in Ulster or elsewhere is to rule the question at large for Ireland, when five-sixths of its chosen representatives are of one mind on the matter."

(From Gladstone's speech in the House of Commons, 8 April 1886.)

SOURCE 37

Should the dog wag the tail, or the tail wag the dog ?

A cartoon published by the Home Rule Council at the time of the Third Home Rule Bill, 1912.

QUESTIONS

5.8 What evidence is there in Source 36 that Gladstone sympathized with the Unionists?

5.9 Why, then, was he ignoring their opposition to Home Rule?

5.10 Explain the meaning of Source 37. In what way does it support Source 36?

The defeat of the Home Rule Bill in the House of Commons in June 1886 was greeted with celebrations in Unionist areas and there was a renewal of sectarian rioting in the summer of 1886. At one stage the army had to be called in to restore order, and by the end of the summer, 32 people had been killed, 442 arrested and 377 police injured.

SOURCE 38

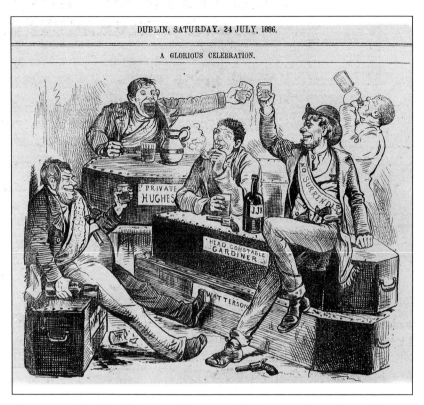

A cartoon entitled "A Glorious Celebration" which appeared in "The Weekly News", 24 July 1886.

5.11 What evidence is there in Source 38, to suggest that the men shown are Orangemen?

5.12 What is the cartoonist suggesting about the results of their "celebrations"?

5.13 Do you feel that the cartoon is reliable historical evidence? Give reasons for your answer.

THE SECOND HOME RULE BILL 1893

By 1892 there were 23 Unionist M.P.s, 19 of them from Ulster, and when Gladstone became Prime Minister again in that year, a number of Unionist Clubs were formed throughout Ulster.

The **Second Home Rule Bill** was passed by the House of Commons, but it was defeated in the House of Lords, giving further cause for Unionist celebration.

TO THE
UNIONISTS OF BALLYMENA
AND NEIGHBOURHOOD.

IN the event of the Home Rule Bill, now before the House of Lords, being thrown out as expected, this Friday night. it is requested that all Unionists will have their Windows Illuminated in honour of its defeat on Saturday night, 9th September.

JOHN PAUL,

89   **District Master, Ballymena.**

An advertisement placed in the "Ballymena Observer", a County Antrim weekly paper, in September 1893.

QUESTIONS

5.14 Does this newspaper advertisement *prove* that Unionists opposed Home Rule?

5.15 What other information would you need to show the degree of Unionist support for Mr. Paul's request?

5.16 Is there any evidence that John Paul was an Orangeman?

Ulster Unionists tightened their control on the Unionist movement with the formation in 1905 of the **Ulster Unionist Council**, at a meeting in the Ulster Hall, Belfast. It consisted of 200 members, drawn from the local Unionist Associations, the Orange Order, Ulster Unionist M.P.s and peers. However, by 1910, still only 21 of the 105 Irish seats in the House of Commons were held by Unionists—18 of them in Ulster.

It was in that year that the Unionists chose as their leader, **Sir Edward Carson**, M.P. for Dublin University, and it was he who led Unionist opposition to the Third Home Rule Bill, which was introduced into the House of Commons in 1912 by H. H. Asquith, the Prime Minister and Liberal Party leader since 1908.

6 The Ulster Crisis 1912-1914

THE THIRD HOME RULE BILL 1912

After ten years of Conservative rule, the Liberals returned to power in December 1905. The General Election gave them a large majority and in 1907 Henry Campbell-Bannerman, the Prime Minister, proposed setting up an Irish Council, a compromise between the Nationalist and Unionist positions. However, in the face of opposition from both the Nationalists and the Unionists, the Bill was dropped.

In 1908 Campbell-Bannerman was succeeded as Prime Minister by **H. H. Asquith**, and at the end of 1909, he declared his support for Home Rule. However, the General Election of December 1910 left the Liberals without an overall majority.

Date	Liberal	Conservative/Unionist	Labour	Irish Nationalist
1906	400	157	30	83
1910	272	272	42	84

(General Election results of January 1906 and December 1910.)

6.1 Why would the Liberals have been more likely to introduce a Home Rule Bill after 1910 than before 1910?

Ever since 1905, the Conservative majority in the House of Lords had been rejecting government Bills passed by the House of Commons, and so, in 1910, with the support of the Irish Nationalist Party, led by **John Redmond**, Asquith introduced a Parliament Bill, which, when it was passed in 1911, reduced the power of the House of Lords. Instead of being able to defeat a Bill, the Lords could do no more than delay it for two years.

In April 1912, Asquith introduced the **Third Home Rule Bill** into the House of Commons. With the support of the Irish Nationalists and with the power of the House of Lords reduced, the Bill was almost certain to become law in 1914. The Unionists in Ireland were determined that it should not.

John Dillon and John Redmond, leaders of the Irish Nationalist Party.

A cartoon showing Redmond trying in vain to herd all of Ireland through the "Home Rule Gate".

6.2 Why is one of the pigs refusing to go through the gate?

6.3 In the cartoon, could "North-east Ulster" harm Redmond? Could North-east Ulster harm Redmond in real life?

6.4 Compare the photograph of Redmond in Source 41 with the cartoonist's version of him. Comment on the way he is depicted in the cartoon.

SOURCE 43

"An act to amend the provision for the government of Ireland....

1 (1) ... there shall be in Ireland an Irish parliament consisting of his majesty the king and two houses, namely the Irish Senate and the Irish House of Commons.

 (2) ... the supreme power and authority of the parliament of the United Kingdom shall remain unaffected....

2   ... the Irish parliament shall have power to make laws for the peace, order, and good government of Ireland ... they shall not have power to make any laws except in matters exclusively relating to Ireland ... they shall not have power to make laws in respect of the following matters ...

(1) The crown....

(2) The making of peace and war....

(3) ... the defence of the realm....

(4) Treaties ... with foreign states....

(5) ... titles of honour....

(6) Treason....

(7) Trade with any place out of Ireland....

[and other similar restrictions].

3   ... the Irish parliament shall not make a law ... to establish or endow any religion, or prohibit or restrict the free exercise thereof ..."

[There followed other detailed clauses, and the Act concluded with:]

41   The Irish parliament shall not have power to repeal or alter any provision of this act ... or of any act passed by the parliament of the United Kingdom...."

(Extract from the Government of Ireland Act, as it was passed in 1914.)

6.5 Explain in your own words what the Act proposed.

6.6 Compare Source 43 with Source 27. How far did the Government of Ireland Act meet the demands of the Home Rule Conference of 1873?

6.7 What would you expect to be the attitude to the Government of Ireland Act of:

(a) the Irish Nationalists?

(b) the Unionists?

(c) the Irish Republican Brotherhood?

Explain your answer in each case.

OPPOSITION TO HOME RULE

Sir Edward Carson, the Unionist leader, knew that the Home Rule Bill could not be defeated in Parliament, but he felt that if the Ulster Unionists opposed it strongly enough, the government could be forced to drop the proposal. Carson believed that Home Rule would be bad for the whole of Ireland, although many of his supporters, including **James Craig**, M.P. for East Down, saw the problem as purely an Ulster one, and many were prepared to see

Ireland divided with Ulster remaining outside the control of the Home Rule Parliament in Dublin.

The Unionists still had the support of the Conservatives, and **Andrew Bonar Law**, the Conservative leader, spoke in support of the Unionist position.

SOURCE 44

"... They may, perhaps they will, carry their Home Rule Bill through the House of Commons, but what then? I said the other day in the House of Commons and I repeat here that there are things stronger than parliamentary majorities.

... Before I occupied the position I now fill in the party I said that in my belief, if an attempt were made to deprive these men of their birthright ... they would be justified in resisting such an attempt by all means in their power, including force.... If such an attempt is made, I can imagine no lengths of resistance to which Ulster can go in which I should not be prepared to support them, and in which, in my belief, they would not be supported by the overwhelming majority of the British people."

(Bonar Law speaking at a mass meeting in the grounds of Blenheim Palace, the home of the Duke of Marlborough, in England, in July 1912.)

QUESTIONS

6.8 Whom does Bonar Law mean by "they" in the first line?

6.9 What does he mean by "there are things stronger than parliamentary majorities"?

6.10 Are you surprised by any parts of this speech? If so, why?

Now look through Sources 45(A) to 51, which provide some evidence of the actions taken by the Unionists in an effort to prevent Home Rule from becoming law, or at least to prevent it from being put into effect in Ulster.

QUESTIONS

6.11 Make a list of the different actions taken by the Unionists.

6.12 Which of their actions do you think would have attracted most support on the British mainland?

6.13 Make a list of the different types of historical source used in Sources 45 to 51. Can you think of any other types of source which would help you to understand the actions of the Unionists?

6.14 What evidence is there to support Bonar Law's phrase "by all means in their power"?

SOURCE 45

(A) "We must be prepared, in the event of a Home Rule Bill passing, with such measures as will carry on for ourselves the government of those districts of which we have control. We must be prepared ... the morning Home Rule passes, ourselves to become responsible for the government of the Protestant Province of Ulster."

(Sir Edward Carson addressing a gathering of 50 000 Orangemen and other Unionists in the grounds of James Craig's home near Belfast, on 23 September 1911, even before the Home Rule Bill had been introduced into Parliament.)

(B)

ULSTER
PROVISIONAL GOVERNMENT
PROCLAMATION

TO ALL WHOM IT MAY CONCERN.

WHEREAS ULSTERMEN, Free Citizens of a United Kingdom, Born into Possession of Full Rights and Privileges under ONE KING and ONE IMPERIAL PARLIAMENT, are threatened with the calamity of being deprived of their Birthright and being Forcibly Subjected to a Nationalist Parliament and Executive, regardless of their steadfast allegiance in the past to their King and Empire.

BE IT KNOWN

That, for the Public Safety and Security of Civil and Religious Liberty to All Classes and Creeds, duly-elected Delegates and Covenanters representative of all parts of Ulster, in the City of Belfast this day assembled, finally settled the form of

PROVISIONAL GOVERNMENT

WITHIN THE PROVINCE OF ULSTER.

THE DATE upon which it shall become effective, together with instructions regarding all other matters necessary for Repudiating and Resisting the Decrees of such Nationalist Parliament or Executive and for taking over the Government of the Province IN TRUST for the British Nation will be made public as and when it shall be deemed expedient.

ON BEHALF OF THE CENTRAL AUTHORITY.

EDWARD CARSON.
LONDONDERRY.
ABERCORN.
JOHN YOUNG.
THOMAS SINCLAIR.
THOMAS ANDREWS.

OLD TOWN HALL, BELFAST, 24th SEPTEMBER, 1913.

GOD SAVE THE KING.

A poster, dated 24 September 1912, announcing that details of how a Provisional Government would operate, had been worked out.

QUESTIONS

6.15 What is meant by a "Provisional Government"?

6.16 When according to Source 45A was it to be put into effect?

SOURCE 46

(A)

Ulster's
Solemn League and Covenant.

Being convinced in our consciences that Home Rule would be disastrous to the material well-being of Ulster as well as of the whole of Ireland, subversive of our civil and religious freedom, destructive of our citizenship and perilous to the unity of the Empire, we, whose names are under-written, men of Ulster, loyal subjects of His Gracious Majesty King George V., humbly relying on the God whom our fathers in days of stress and trial confidently trusted, do hereby pledge ourselves in solemn Covenant throughout this our time of threatened calamity to stand by one another in defending for ourselves and our children our cherished position of equal citizen-ship in the United Kingdom and in using all means which may be found necessary to defeat the present conspiracy to set up a Home Rule Parliament in Ireland. ¶ And in the event of such a Parliament being forced upon us we further solemnly and mutually pledge ourselves to refuse to recognise its authority. ¶ In sure confidence that God will defend the right we hereto subscribe our names. ¶ And further, we individually declare that we have not already signed this Covenant.

The above was signed by me at ~in my own hand~ The City Hall Belfast at "Ulster Day." Saturday, 28th September, 1912. 3·45 pm

Fred H. Crawford   Chlorine Gardens, 20 mill st   Belfast

God Save the King.

This document was signed by 218 206 men throughout Ulster in September 1912. Many signed it in their own blood. Women were not invited to sign but 228 991 women signed a separate declaration pledging their support.

(B)

The Ulster Hall, Belfast Friday 27 September 1912. An artist's impression of the scene at the Unionist rally outside the Ulster Hall, the evening before the Covenant was signed.

6.17 Explain in your own words the reasons given in the first four and a half lines of Source 46 for the Unionists' opposition to Home Rule.

6.18 What similarity can you find between this document and Bonar Law's speech (Source 44)?

6.19 In what ways could those who signed this Covenant be described as (a) loyal? and (b) rebellious?

6.20 Try to find out what was the first "Solemn League and Covenant".

SOURCE 47 (A)

A poster advertising a demonstration against Home Rule, to be held in Belfast on 19 January, 1914.

(B)

Sir Edward Carson addressing one of the many anti-Home Rule rallies held in Ulster during the period 1912 to 1914.

SOURCE 48

The Ulster Volunteer Force (U.V.F.) was set up in January 1913 by the Ulster Unionist Council. It was financed by Ulster businessmen and by English supporters. Lord Rothschild, the Duke of Bedford and Rudyard Kipling were among those who sent thousands of pounds. The U.V.F. was commanded by Sir George Richardson and was trained by army officers. Membership was restricted to 100 000 men who had signed the Covenant. The U.V.F. was permitted to drill when given the authority to do so by two magistrates.

6.21 Do you think the U.V.F. would have had difficulty finding two magistrates to give them permission to drill?

(A)

An artist's impression of the scene at Larne, County Antrim on the night of 24 April 1914, when guns were smuggled in for the Ulster Volunteer Force.

(B)

An artist's view of a similar scene at Donaghadee, County Down.

The Ulster Unionist Council authorized Lt. Col. Frederick Crawford, a founder member of the U.V.F., to purchase guns in Hamburg, Germany. 35 000 guns and 5 000 000 rounds of ammunition were smuggled into Ulster on the night of 24–25 April 1914.

(C)

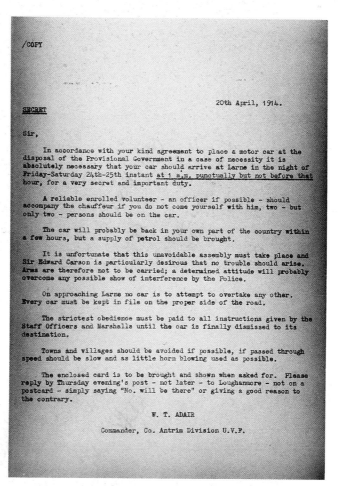

A secret memorandum dated 20 April 1914, giving details of how the gun-running was to be carried out. It is signed by General Sir William Adair, a retired British army officer, who was in charge of the Larne gun-running.

6.22 Do you think Sources 49(A) and (B) are reliable sources of historical evidence?

6.23 In what way do Sources 49(A) and (B) support Source 49(C)?

6.24 Do you think the Unionists were justified in smuggling guns into Ulster to resist an Act of Parliament?

SOURCE 50

(A)

A Unionist postcard featuring an artist's humorous interpretation of how the centre of Belfast would look if Home Rule came into force. The City Hall is falling down, the shops are to let, a statue of Queen Victoria has been replaced by one of John Redmond, and there are cows grazing in the middle of the street.

(B)

(C)

*Three more postcards published by the Unionists at this time **(B)**, **(C)**, and **(D)**.*

(D)

QUESTIONS

6.25 What is the value of these postcards to a historian?

6.26 Why do you think they were published?

SOURCE 51

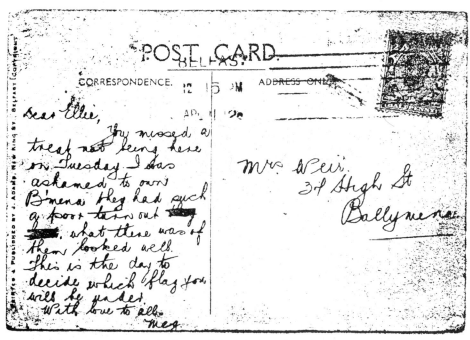

A postcard sent by a lady who had attended an anti-Home Rule rally in Belfast.

6.27 To whom do you think "Meg" was referring when she said, "What there was of them looked well"?

6.28 What can you learn from this postcard about "Meg's" attitude to Home Rule?

6.29 In what ways is this postcard useful to a historian?

Despite all this Unionist activity, the Home Rule Bill made its way through the various stages in Parliament. Carson and the other Unionist M.P.s continued to argue that the position of Ulster should be given special consideration.

"The speech from the throne talks of the fears of these men. Yes, they have, I think, genuine fears for their civil and religious liberty under the Bill, but do not imagine that that is all that these men are fighting for. They are fighting for a great principle, and a great ideal. They are fighting to stay under a government which they were invited to come under, under which they have flourished, and under which they are content, and to refuse to come under a government which they loathe and detest. Men do not make sacrifices or take up the attitude these men of Ulster have taken up on a question of detail or paper safeguards. I am not going to argue whether they are right or wrong in resisting. It would be useless to argue it, because they have thoroughly made up their minds, but I say this: if these men are not morally justified when they are attempted to be driven out of one government with which they are satisfied and put under another which they loathe, I do not see how resistance ever can be justified in history at all."

(An extract from a speech by Sir Edward Carson in February 1914.)

6.30 What is meant by "the speech from the throne"?

6.31 To whom does Carson refer when he says "these men"?

6.32 What were "these men" afraid of?

6.33 Why does Carson feel that they are justified in resisting the law?

THE NATIONALIST REACTION

Eoin MacNeill and the Irish Volunteers

In November 1913 **Eoin MacNeill**, Professor of Irish History at University College Dublin and a founder of the Gaelic League, wrote an article entitled "The North Began", in *An Claidheamh Soluis*. In it he praised the Ulster Volunteers for taking steps to protect their own interests and he suggested that the Nationalists should take similar steps to achieve their aims. Bulmer Hobson then arranged a public meeting in Dublin on 25 November 1913, which resulted in the formation of the **Irish Volunteer Force (I.V.F.)**, with MacNeill as Chief of Staff. It attracted members from the Gaelic League, the Gaelic Athletic Association, Sinn Féin, and the Irish Republican Brotherhood, which hoped to use the I.V.F. for its own purposes. By May 1914 there were around 80 000 members.

A 1913 recruiting poster for the Irish Volunteers.

6.34 What can you learn about the aims of the Irish Volunteers from the wording of Source 53?

John Redmond was alarmed at the existence of such a large organization totally outside his control and so he demanded, and received, 25 seats on the Committee, for the Irish Parliamentary Party.

The I.V.F., following the example of the Ulster Volunteers, also sent representatives to Germany to buy guns, and on 26 July 1914, 900 rifles and 29 000 rounds of ammunition were landed at **Howth**, near Dublin, in broad daylight.

A photograph of the landing of guns for the Irish Volunteers at Howth on 26 July 1914.

6.35 Can you suggest any reasons why the Irish Volunteers smuggled in their guns during daylight?

The authorities sent troops to seize the weapons, but the attempt failed, and on the way back to their barracks, the soldiers were jeered at by a crowd. The soldiers opened fire and three civilians were killed.

This incident, at **Bachelor's Walk**, caused great anger, not least because no action had been taken against the U.V.F. gun-runners three months earlier.

James Connolly and the Citizen Army

A third private army was set up in Ireland in 1913, which at first seemed to have more to do with the living conditions of the working people of Dublin than it did with Irish politics.

"One-third of all Dublin people lived in terrible slums. Over two thousand families lived in one-room tenements [i.e. flats] without water, light or sanitation. Three-quarters of the men were unskilled labourers and about fifteen per cent were unemployed. For those who had work the average pay was only £1 a week, though it was calculated that at least 22/6 [£1-12½] a week was necessary to feed a family. The result was that people were always undernourished, very subject to disease, especially tuberculosis (T.B.), and sought in drink an escape from their misery. Dublin had one of the highest death rates in Europe."

(An account of the living conditions of the poor in Dublin at the beginning of the 20th century, from *Ireland 1800–1970* by M. E. Collins, published in 1976.)

6.36 Source 55 was written 70 years after the situation it describes. Does that make it unreliable historical evidence? How could a historian check its reliability?

6.37 Who do you think was to blame for the dreadful conditions described in Source 55?

6.38 Do you think that the people described in Source 55 would have been more interested or less interested in political issues such as Home Rule than the more prosperous Dubliners?

In an effort to improve these conditions, **Jim Larkin** set up the Irish Transport and General Workers' Union in 1908. He was assisted by **James Connolly**, and over the next few years the union did force some employers to improve wages and conditions.

However in August 1913, the employers made an attempt to destroy Larkin's union, when they tried to force their workers to leave the union. When the workers refused, 25 000 of them were "locked out" by their employers. Dublin was brought almost to a standstill for six months. In the end, despite support from trade unionists in England, the men and women had to return to work on the employers' terms.

During the "lock-out", violent police behaviour at demonstrations by workers led Larkin to ask "If it is right and legal for the men of Ulster to arm, why should it not be right and legal for the men of Dublin to arm themselves to protect themselves?"

So in November 1913, the **Irish Citizen Army** was formed, at first under the command of Captain Jack White D.S.O., a Protestant from Broughshane, County Antrim, and a former British army officer. In 1914 James Connolly replaced White as Commander, and under Connolly's leadership, the Citizen Army developed two clear aims—to gain independence for Ireland, and to establish a socialist republic in which working-class Irish people of all religions would join together. Although it was never a large organization— around 200—the Citizen Army had quite a lot of influence and it drew the attention of other Nationalists to the conditions of the poor in Dublin.

SOURCE 56

A leaflet, published in 1913, explaining the aims of the Irish Citizen Army.

6.39 Find out the meaning of "socialist".

6.40 Compare Source 56 with Source 53. In what ways are the aims of the Irish Volunteers (a) similar? and (b) different?

6.41 What evidence is there in Source 56 that the Citizen Army was *both* a nationalist *and* a socialist organization?

THE CURRAGH MUTINY

The formation of these armed groups in the south did not worry the government as much as did the Ulster Volunteer Force in the north. The Home Rule Bill was due to become law in September 1914, and in the face of continued Unionist opposition, plans were made for the protection of arms depots in Ulster. Army officers from Ulster were told that they would not be expected to serve in their home province, but the other officers were asked to give an assurance that they were willing to serve there, and they were told that if they refused, they faced dismissal. Fifty-eight officers stationed at **The Curragh**, the Military Headquarters in Ireland, said that they would prefer to be dismissed rather than take action against the Unionists in Ulster.

They were not dismissed and the whole affair was patched up, but it showed that the army might prove unreliable, and that further discussion might offer the best hope of avoiding civil war.

6.42 What effect would the Curragh "Mutiny" have had on (a) the Unionists? and (b) the supporters of Home Rule?

THE BUCKINGHAM PALACE CONFERENCE

In July 1914, Asquith, Redmond, Bonar Law, Carson and Craig were among those who met at **Buckingham Palace**, at the request of King George V, to discuss the possibility of excluding part of Ulster from the Home Rule Bill.

However, neither the Unionists nor the Nationalists were prepared to make any concession and the conference broke up after three days. Ireland appeared to be on the brink of civil war.

THE FIRST WORLD WAR

Then on 4 August 1914, Britain entered the **First World War**, following a German invasion of Belgium, and although the Home Rule Bill received the Royal Assent and so became law on 18 September, it was suspended until six months after the end of the war. Carson and Redmond agreed to this and they both promised their full support for the war effort.

7 Ireland and the First World War

SUPPORT FOR THE WAR

There were several different attitudes, among the Irish leaders, to the involvement of Irishmen on the side of Britain in the First World War.

As one might expect, Sir Edward Carson, the Unionist leader, saw the war as an opportunity for Unionists to show their loyalty. He hoped that it would entitle Ulster to special treatment after the war, and he convinced the authorities to absorb the Ulster Volunteers into the British army as a distinct unit—the **36th (Ulster) Division**.

John Redmond, the leader of the Irish Nationalists, explained his point of view to the Irish Volunteers on 20 September 1914.

SOURCE 57

"The duty of the manhood of Ireland is twofold. Its duty is, at all costs, to defend the shores of Ireland against foreign invasion. It is a duty more than that, of taking care that Irish valour proves itself on the field of war as it has always proved itself in the past.

The interests of Ireland—of the whole of Ireland—are at stake in this war. The war is undertaken in defence of the highest principles of religion and morality and right, and it would be a disgrace for ever to our country ... if young Ireland confined their efforts to remaining at home to defend the shores of Ireland from an unlikely invasion, and shrunk from the duty of proving on the field of battle that gallantry and courage which has distinguished our race all through its history.

I say to you, therefore, your duty is twofold.... I say to you, 'Go on drilling and make yourselves efficient for the work, and then account yourselves as men, not only in Ireland itself, but wherever the firing-line extends, in defence of right, of freedom, and of religion in this war.'"

(Redmond addressing an Irish Volunteer parade in County Wicklow, 20 September 1914.)

SOURCE 58

An Irish recruiting poster, 1914.

SOURCE 59

WILL **YOU** ANSWER THE CALL?

NOW IS THE TIME,

AND THE PLACE IS THE NEAREST RECRUIT...

JAMES WALKER (Dublin) L™ DUBLIN.   W.T.P. 67.7.300 6/18

An Irish recruiting poster, 1914.

UESTIONS

7.1 What does Redmond want Irishmen to do during the war? What reasons does he give in Source 57?

7.2 Do you think that all Nationalists in Ireland would have agreed with him? Give reasons for your answer.

7.3 In what ways do Sources 58 and 59 support Source 57?

The majority of the Irish Volunteers accepted Redmond's point of view, believing that their support for the war effort would guarantee Home Rule for Ireland after the war. However, these **National Volunteers**, as they became known, were not kept together as a separate unit in the army, in the way the Ulster Volunteers were.

As well as these new volunteers, there were of course several Irish regiments in the regular army.

36th (Ulster) Division

107th Brigade
8th Royal Irish Rifles
    (East Belfast Volunteers)
9th Royal Irish Rifles
    (West Belfast Volunteers)
10th Royal Irish Rifles
    (South Belfast Volunteers)
15th Royal Irish Rifles
    (North Belfast Volunteers)

108th Brigade
11th Royal Irish Rifles
    (South Antrim Volunteers)
12th Royal Irish Rifles
    (Mid Antrim Volunteers)
13th Royal Irish Rifles
    (1st County Down Volunteers)
9th Royal Irish Fusiliers
    (Armagh, Monaghan and Cavan
        Volunteers)

109th Brigade
9th Royal Inniskilling Fusiliers
    (Tyrone Volunteers)
10th Royal Inniskilling Fusiliers
    (Derry Volunteers)
11th Royal Inniskilling Fusiliers
    (Donegal and Fermanagh Volunteers)
14th Royal Irish Rifles
    (Belfast Young Citizen Volunteers)
Pioneer Battalion—16th Royal Irish Rifles
                (2nd County Down Volunteers)

10th (Irish) Division

29th Brigade
5th Royal Irish Regiment
6th Royal Irish Rifles
5th Connaught Rangers
6th Leinster Regiment

30th Brigade
6th Royal Dublin Fusiliers
7th Royal Dublin Fusiliers
6th Royal Munster Fusiliers
7th Royal Munster Fusiliers

31st Brigade
5th Royal Inniskilling Fusiliers
6th Royal Inniskilling Fusiliers
5th Royal Irish Fusiliers
6th Royal Irish Fusiliers

(Some of the Irish battalions in the British army during the First World War.)

Almost 250 000 Irishmen fought in the First World War and perhaps as many as 60 000 did not return. The 16th (Irish) Division, which contained many National Volunteers, lost over 5000 men at Gallipoli in 1915, and the 36th (Ulster) Division, which was made up almost entirely of U.V.F. members, lost 5500 in one day—1 July 1916, the first day of the Battle of the Somme. That day, four Ulstermen won the Victoria Cross, and altogether eleven V.C.s were won by Irishmen during the war. The 16th and 36th Divisions fought side by side at the Battle of Messines in 1917.

One of a series of Christmas postcards, painted by the Ulster artist, William Conor, and sold to raise funds for the U.V.F. hospitals for the wounded.

Charge of the Ulster Division.

Legend has it that it was an Irishman, Private Ernest Thomas from Tipperary, of the Royal Irish Dragoons, who fired the first shot at the Germans, eighteen days after Britain entered the war, and that it was an Irishman, Private W. Ellison of the Royal Irish Lancers, who was the last man to die in the war, at the very moment of the ceasefire, 11 a.m. on 11 November 1918.

7.4 Is there enough evidence in this chapter to support the statement "Irishmen played a major part in the First World War"?

7.5 What other sources of evidence would a historian need to enable him to accept that statement?

OPPOSITION TO IRISH INVOLVEMENT

However, not everyone believed that Irishmen should support the war effort.

"Full steam ahead, John Redmond said,
That everything was well, chum;
Home Rule will come when we are dead
And buried out in Belgium."

(From the weekly newspaper *Workers' Republic*, founded by James Connolly, 6 November 1915.)

James **Connolly**, as a socialist, saw no reason for the Irish working classes to kill the German working classes, and as an Irishman, he saw the war as England's war; Ireland, he said, had no quarrel with Germany.
    Arthur Griffith, of Sinn Féin, agreed.

"Ireland is not at war with Germany.... England is at war with Germany.... Our duty is in no doubt. We are Irish Nationalists and the only duty we can have is to stand for Ireland's interests."

(Arthur Griffith's attitude to the War, 1914.)

"For hail or rain or frost or snow,
We're not going out to Flanders, O,
While there's fighting to be done at home.
Let your privates and commanders go.
Let Englishmen for England fight;
It's nearly time they started, O!"

(An anonymous Irish ballad of the time.)

Q UESTIONS

7.6 Explain in your own words the meaning of Source 61.
7.7 Does the writer of Source 63 agree with Redmond in Source 57, or with Griffith in Source 62?
7.8 In Source 63, explain the meaning of the reference to "Flanders".
7.9 What do you think is meant by the third line of Source 63?

A section of the Irish Volunteers also refused to support Redmond's call. Around 11 000 men reorganized under MacNeill's leadership, and they kept the title **Irish Volunteers**, while Redmond's supporters became known as the **National Volunteers**. Most of MacNeill's Irish Volunteers believed that they should build up their strength to ensure that Home Rule was put into effect after the war.

However, those who were also members of the Irish Republican Brotherhood—men such as Thomas Clarke, Seán MacDermott and Patrick Pearse—wanted to use the Volunteers in a rebellion against Britain. They thought that "England's difficulty was Ireland's opportunity". They believed that even if the rebellion was a failure, their deaths might revive Irish patriotism.

Preparations were soon under way for the Easter Rising of 1916.

8

The Easter Rising 1916

PREPARATIONS

Patrick Pearse, a member of the Gaelic League, the Irish Volunteers and the I.R.B., was the man who most clearly expressed the feelings of those who supported the idea of a rebellion during the First World War.

"Ireland unarmed will attain just as much freedom as it is convenient for England to give her; Ireland armed will attain ultimately just as much freedom as she wants.... I am glad that the North has 'begun'. I am glad to see the Orangemen armed, for it is a goodly thing to see arms in Irish hands.... I should like to see any and every body of Irish citizens armed. We must accustom ourselves to the thought of arms, to the sight of arms, to the use of arms. We may make mistakes in the beginning and shoot the wrong people; but bloodshed is a cleansing and a sanctifying thing, and the nation which regards it as the final horror has lost its manhood. There are many things more horrible than bloodshed; and slavery is one of them."

(From *The Coming Revolution* by Patrick Pearse, November 1913.)

8.1 Explain in your own words Pearse's attitude to the use of violence.

8.2 What reasons does he give in the first sentence of Source 64 for supporting the use of violence? Do you think what he said in that sentence was true?

8.3 Do you think that all those who were opposed to British rule in Ireland at that time would have agreed with Pearse? Can you name an Irish Nationalist leader who was opposed to the use of violence for political purposes?

Pearse became obsessed with the idea that a "**blood-sacrifice**" by Irishmen would encourage others to fight for the freedom of Ireland.

"Life springs from death; and from the graves of patriot men and women spring living nations. The Defenders of this Realm have worked well in secret and in the open. They think they have pacified Ireland. They think they have purchased half of us and intimidated [i.e. frightened] the other half. They think that they have foreseen everything, think they have provided against everything; but the fools, the fools, the fools!—they have left us our Fenian dead, and while Ireland holds these graves, Ireland unfree shall never be at peace.

(Part of Patrick Pearse's speech at the funeral of Jeremiah O'Donovan Rossa, an old Fenian, who died in August 1915.)

8.4 To whom does Pearse refer when he speaks of "The Defenders of this Realm"? What does he say they think they have done?

8.5 Try to explain in your own words what Pearse means in his first sentence and in his last sentence.

Thomas Clarke and Seán MacDermott, leading members of the Irish Republican Brotherhood, had been planning a rebellion since 1914. In 1915, the I.R.B. formed a **Military Council**, consisting of Clarke, MacDermott, Pearse, Joseph Plunkett and Éamonn Ceannt. They were later joined by Thomas MacDonagh. Although several of these men also held high rank in the Irish Volunteers, their plans were not known by Eoin MacNeill, the I.V.F. leader.

In January 1916, this Military Council decided to stage a rising at Easter. James Connolly, who was planning a rebellion of his own, with his 200-strong Citizen Army, was asked to join them. Connolly was confident that the people of Ireland would rise in support.

SOURCE 66

The Irish Citizen Army on parade, outside Liberty Hall, the headquarters of the Irish Transport and General Workers' Union. Connolly had hung the banner above the door shortly after he took command in 1914.

QUESTIONS

8.6 What is the earliest date on which the banner above the door could have been displayed?

8.7 Explain what is meant by the wording on the banner.

8.8 What two aims did James Connolly have?

Sir Roger Casement, a Dublin-born Protestant, who retired from the British diplomatic service in 1913, after a distinguished career, had joined the Irish Volunteers and had been sent to Germany in 1914, to arrange for arms to be shipped to Ireland, and to try to gain German support. The Germans were reluctant to become involved, but in the end they did send 20 000 rifles, which were due to arrive in Ireland shortly before Easter.

The main problem for the Military Council was that **Eoin MacNeill**, the leader of the Volunteers, knew nothing about their plans, and he was certain to oppose them, for he believed that the Irish people did not want a rebellion. He also knew that the Volunteers would be outnumbered by the army, and that only one in five of the Volunteers had a gun. However, without the involvement of the Irish Volunteers, the Rising was certain to fail, because of the small numbers in the Citizen Army and the I.R.B.

On the Wednesday before Easter, MacNeill was shown a document which seemed to show that the authorities were planning to arrest the Volunteers' leaders. Although the document was almost certainly a forgery, this information, along with the news that guns were on their way from Germany, persuaded MacNeill not to interfere, and he allowed the training exercise planned for the Volunteers during the Easter weekend to go ahead. The Citizen Army too was ordered to gather on Easter Sunday.

The government believed that the extreme Nationalists were not strong enough to pose a threat and, because it did not want to provoke them, no attempt had been made to prevent the Irish Volunteers and the Irish Citizen Army from holding regular parades and training exercises.

SOURCE 67

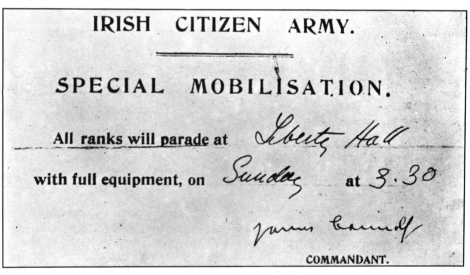

The note, signed by James Connolly, ordering the Citizen Army to parade on Sunday at 3.30.

Just when everything seemed to be going according to plan, disaster struck. On the Friday before Easter, the German ship, *The Aud*, was captured by the British navy. It was scuttled by its Captain and the 20 000 rifles were lost. Almost at the same time, Roger Casement was arrested coming ashore from a German submarine.

Since the government was now bound to know that something was planned, MacNeill cancelled the I.V.F. manoeuvres on the Saturday, and he put an announcement of the cancellation in one of the popular Sunday newspapers. He did not believe that the Rising could succeed and he saw no point in squandering lives unnecessarily.

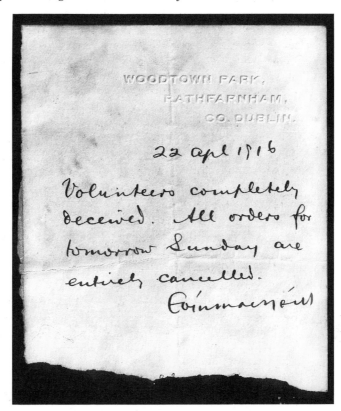

MacNeill's order, dated Saturday 22 April 1916, cancelling the Irish Volunteers' plans for the following day.

"Owing to the very critical position, all orders given to Irish Volunteers for tomorrow, Easter Sunday, are hereby rescinded [i.e. cancelled] and no parades, marches or other movements of Irish Volunteers will take place. Each individual Volunteer will obey this order strictly in every particular."

(MacNeill's announcement which appeared in the *Sunday Independent*, 23 April 1916.)

QUESTIONS

8.9 What piece of information in Source 68 makes it a more useful piece of historical evidence than Source 67?

8.10 Why do you think MacNeill put his announcement in the newspaper on Sunday 23 April (Source 69), when he had already issued the order the previous day (Source 68)?

8.11 What does the first sentence of Source 68 suggest about MacNeill's knowledge of the planned Rising?

8.12 Around 1500 Irish Volunteers took part in the Rising when it eventually took place on Easter Monday. Does that *prove* that they ignored MacNeill's orders?

THE RISING

The Military Council of the I.R.B. met in Liberty Hall on Easter Sunday and decided to postpone the Rising until the following day, using the Irish Citizen Army and their own men in the Irish Volunteers.

And so, on **Easter Monday**, about 1500 rebels occupied a number of important buildings in the centre of Dublin. After the capture of Casement and *The Aud*, the authorities were not expecting any trouble, and since it was a holiday, the city was reasonably quiet.

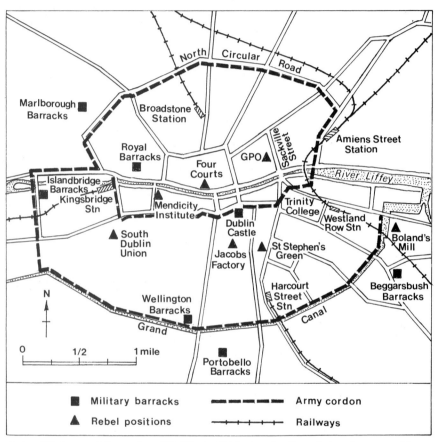

A simplified map of the centre of Dublin in 1916, showing the rebel and army positions.

Pearse, Connolly, Clarke, MacDermott and Plunkett established their Headquarters in the **General Post Office** in Sackville Street (now O'Connell Street), where they raised the green, white and orange tricolour, which had first been seen during the Young Ireland uprising of 1848, and a flag with a golden harp on a green background, bearing the words "Irish Republic" in Gaelic lettering.

Pearse then read the **Proclamation of the Irish Republic** to a puzzled and indifferent crowd. The Proclamation was signed by the seven members of the I.R.B. Military Council, who now called themselves "The Provisional Government".

SOURCE 70

POBLACHT NA H EIREANN.

THE PROVISIONAL GOVERNMENT
OF THE
IRISH REPUBLIC
TO THE PEOPLE OF IRELAND.

IRISHMEN AND IRISHWOMEN : In the name of God and of the dead generations
from which she receives her old tradition of nationhood, Ireland, through us, summons
her children to her flag and strikes for her freedom.

Having organised and trained her manhood through her secret revolutionary
organisation, the Irish Republican Brotherhood, and through her open military
organisations, the Irish Volunteers and the Irish Citizen Army, having patiently
perfected her discipline, having resolutely waited for the right moment to reveal
itself, she now seizes that moment, and, supported by her exiled children in America
and by gallant allies in Europe, but relying in the first on her own strength, she
strikes in full confidence of victory.

We declare the right of the people of Ireland to the ownership of Ireland, and to
the unfettered control of Irish destinies, to be sovereign and indefeasible. The long
usurpation of that right by a foreign people and government has not extinguished the
right, nor can it ever be extinguished except by the destruction of the Irish people. In
every generation the Irish people have asserted their right to national freedom and
sovereignty ; six times during the past three hundred years they have asserted it in
arms. Standing on that fundamental right and again asserting it in arms in the face
of the world, we hereby proclaim the Irish Republic as a Sovereign Independent State,
and we pledge our lives and the lives of our comrades-in-arms to the cause of its freedom,
of its welfare, and of its exaltation among the nations.

The Irish Republic is entitled to, and hereby claims, the allegiance of every
Irishman and Irishwoman. The Republic guarantees religious and civil liberty, equal
rights and equal opportunities to all its citizens, and declares its resolve to pursue
the happiness and prosperity of the whole nation and of all its parts, cherishing all
the children of the nation equally, and oblivious of the differences carefully fostered
by an alien government, which have divided a minority from the majority in the past.

Until our arms have brought the opportune moment for the establishment of a
permanent National Government, representative of the whole people of Ireland and
elected by the suffrages of all her men and women, the Provisional Government, hereby
constituted, will administer the civil and military affairs of the Republic in trust for
the people.

We place the cause of the Irish Republic under the protection of the Most High God,
Whose blessing we invoke upon our arms, and we pray that no one who serves that
cause will dishonour it by cowardice, inhumanity, or rapine. In this supreme hour
the Irish nation must, by its valour and discipline and by the readiness of its children
to sacrifice themselves for the common good, prove itself worthy of the august destiny
to which it is called.

Signed on Behalf of the Provisional Government,
THOMAS J. CLARKE,
SEAN Mac DIARMADA, THOMAS MacDONAGH,
P. H. PEARSE, EAMONN CEANNT,
JAMES CONNOLLY. JOSEPH PLUNKETT.

The Proclamation of the Irish Republic, read by Patrick Pearse on the steps of the G.P.O. in Dublin, on Easter Monday 1916.

QUESTIONS

8.13 Who do you think are meant by:
  (a) "her exiled children in America", and
  (b) "gallant allies in Europe" (paragraph 2)?

8.14 What is meant by "The long usurpation of that right by a foreign people and government" (paragraph 3)?

8.15 Can you find anything in paragraph 4 that might have been included to ease the fears of the Unionists?

8.16 Paragraph 4 begins with the words "The Irish Republic is entitled to, and hereby claims, the allegiance of every Irishman and Irishwoman". You might like to discuss whether or not the Irish people were likely to give their support to this new Irish Republic.

  Bear in mind:
  (a) the attitude of the Unionists;
  (b) the poverty of many of the working classes;
  (c) the fact that all but two of the M.P.s in the south of Ireland were Nationalists;
  (d) the fact that almost a quarter of a million Irishmen were in the British army;
  (e) the fact that out of a population of $4\frac{1}{2}$ million, only about 1500 people took part in the Easter Rising.

The rebels had hoped to capture Dublin Castle, the government headquarters, but they failed, and this enabled the army to cut the city in two. They also threw a military cordon around the city and brought in reinforcements from other parts of Ireland, and from England.

There was no fighting outside Dublin, except for a few minor incidents, and by the Wednesday the rebels were outnumbered by 20 to 1.

"On the Tuesday, the looting of shops was continuing in full swing. Someone who watched, described:
> 'Little guttersnipes wearing high silk hats and new bowlers and straws, who had never worn headgear before; barefooted little devils with legs buried in Wellington boots, unable to bend their knees.'

Another onlooker described the scene:
> 'A saucy girl flipped a fan with a hand wristleted by a thick gold chain; she wore a sable fur coat, the pockets overhung with stockings and pale pink drawers; on her head was a wide black hat to which she had pinned streamers of blue silk ribbon.'"

(From *The Easter Rising and Irish Independence* by E. G. Power, published in 1979.)

SOURCE 72

"From the windows of the Post Office, the insurgent [i.e. rebel] leaders watched first in disbelief, then in horror, as this scene began to develop. Was it possible that so many people—the very people they were offering their lives to emancipate [i.e. free] from British rule—could shamelessly show themselves to be such a disgrace to Ireland?"

(From *Agony at Easter: The 1916 Irish Uprising* by T. M. Coffey, published in 1969.)

QUESTIONS

8.17 In what way does the final paragraph of Source 70 help to explain the feelings of the rebel leaders described in Source 72?

8.18 How does the writer of Source 72 know that the rebel leaders "watched first in horror, then in disbelief"?

SOURCE 73

An artist's impression of the scene inside the G.P.O. towards the end of Easter week, 1916.

The British army brought in artillery, and a gunboat, *Helga*, fired shells from the River Liffey.

QUESTION

8.19 How reliable do you think Source 73 is as historical evidence? Give reasons for your answer.

By Friday, the city centre was in flames, the civilian population was suffering, both from the fighting and from food shortages, and so on Saturday 29 April, Pearse ordered the rebels to surrender. James Connolly, who had been wounded by troops from the Royal Irish Regiment, agreed to the surrender, and it was troops from that same regiment who tore down the flags from the G.P.O.

SOURCE 74

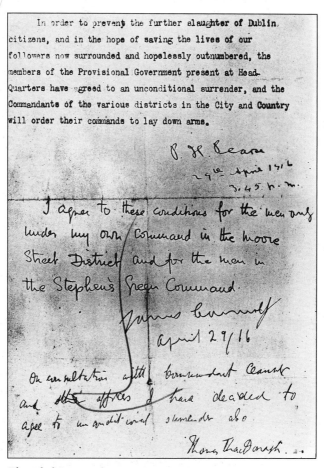

In order to prevent the further slaughter of Dublin citizens, and in the hope of saving the lives of our followers now surrounded and hopelessly outnumbered, the members of the Provisional Government present at Head-Quarters have agreed to an unconditional surrender, and the Commandants of the various districts in the City and Country will order their commands to lay down arms.

The rebels' surrender note.

QUESTION

8.20 What is meant by "unconditional" surrender?

During the **Easter Rising**, which had lasted less than a week, approximately 450 people had been killed, including over 100 British soldiers and over a dozen policemen. Over 2500 people had been wounded. One estimate put the damage caused at £2½ million.

Two views of the General Post Office in Sackville Street after the Easter Rising.

SOURCE 75

"To some people, the way the Volunteers had fought, shooting from rooftops and from behind walls, was cowardly and unfair. People said that shooting unarmed Dublin Metropolitan Policemen was unsporting. Three men of the D.M.P. had been shot. From the other point of view, using artillery against men armed only with rifles was also seen as unfair; and the authorities did other bad things which came out later. In one case, three journalists were arrested, shot and buried at a military barracks on the orders of a British officer, who was later pronounced guilty of murder, but insane. In another, British soldiers searching houses near the Four Courts were accused of shooting fifteen unarmed civilians. When a search was made, two bodies were found in a shallow grave in a cellar. The troops in action in that district were questioned, but nothing definite was found out."

(From *The Easter Rising and Irish Independence* by E. G. Power, published in 1979.)

QUESTIONS

8.21 Bearing in mind the points made in Source 75, you might like to discuss whether you feel that the behaviour of either side was "unfair". Do you think that the behaviour of either side was worse than that of the other?

8.22 Is a book written by a modern historian, such as the one from which Source 75 was taken, likely to be more reliable or less reliable than a book written at the time?

As the rebels were marched away by the soldiers, they were surrounded by a crowd of Dubliners, who were hostile towards the rebels, not towards the British soldiers.

SOURCE 76

"A raucous crowd came pouring out of the houses and out of the side streets to accost them. Here were the looters-turned-patriots. Waving British flags ... [they shouted] 'Murderer!' 'Guttersnipes!' The flood of insults was ... fierce.... The insults of their British conquerors had been easy to take because they had been expected, but these people ... were the very people for whose freedom the insurgents had just been risking death.... One man, marching beside Jim Ryan ... was silent for a while. Then he turned to Ryan once more.

'Do you think they might let us go?' he asked.

Ryan glanced out at the furious fist-shaking crowd, then he broke into a wry Irish smile. 'Bejasus,' he said, 'I hope not'."

(From *Agony at Easter: The 1916 Irish Uprising* by T. M. Coffey, published in 1969.)

8.23 What does the writer of Source 76 mean by "looters-turned-patriots"?

8.24 How do you explain the hostile attitude of the Dublin people?

8.25 Why did Ryan say that he hoped the British would not let him go? Do you think he was serious?

BRITISH TREATMENT OF THE REBELS

Military courts were set up immediately, in which 170 men and one woman were tried by court-martial. Ninety were sentenced to death, but in the end only 15 were executed, by firing-squad, within twelve days of the Rising, including all seven signatories of the Proclamation of the Irish Republic. James Connolly had been so badly wounded during the Rising that he had to be strapped into a chair before he was shot. Roger Casement was convicted of high treason and he was hanged in London in August. Almost 1900 others were imprisoned, or interned without trial, including many Sinn Féin members who had taken no part in the Rising.

Thomas Clarke

Seán MacDermott

Patrick Pearse

Thomas McDonagh

Éamonn Ceantt

The seven members of the Military Council of the I.R.B., and signatories of the Proclamation of the Irish Republic, who were executed in May 1916.

James Connolly

Joseph Plunkett

REBEL LEADERS SURRENDER.

THREE PRINCIPALS TRIED AND SHOT.

OTHERS ARRESTED & HELD FOR TRIAL UNCONDITIONALLY.

SERIOUS FIGHTING ALL ROUND THE CITY

HEAVY CASUALTIES IN DEAD AND WOUNDED.

CENTRE OF DUBLIN DEVASTATED BY FIRE; PALATIAL BUILDINGS IN ASHES.

The Sinn Fein insurrection, which broke out in Dublin City on Easter Monday at noon, has been effectively quelled.

The positions of vantage which the rebels took up in various parts of the city were reduced, and the leaders unconditionally surrendered.

Thomas J. Clarke, P. H. Pearse, and Thomas Macdonagh, three of the signatories to the notice proclaiming an Irish Republic, have been tried by court-martial and

A headline from the "Irish Independent" newspaper, on 4 May 1916.

Liberty Hall, headquarters of the Citizen Army, after the Rising. It had been shelled from the River Liffey, by the gunboat "Helga".

8.26 Comment on the difference between the wording of Source 77 and the words on the banner in Source 78.

"... We seem to have lost, we have not lost. To refuse to fight would have been to lose, to fight is to win, we have kept faith with the past and handed a tradition to the future.... If our deed has not been sufficient to win freedom, then our children will win it by a better deed."

(Patrick Pearse at his court-martial, 2 May 1916.)

"I write it out in verse—
MacDonagh and MacBride
And Connolly and Pearse
Now and in time to be,
Wherever green is worn,
Are changed, changed utterly;
A terrible beauty is born."

(An extract from *Easter 1916*, a poem by W. B. Yeats.)

ⓠ UESTIONS

8.27 What does Pearse mean in Source 79, by "we have kept faith with the past and handed a tradition to the future"?

8.28 Pearse was tried in secret. How do you think his speech at his trial became publicly known? Do you think he intended his words to be made public? If so, why?

8.29 In what way does Pearse's statement in Source 79 help to explain the last line of Yeats' poem in Source 80?

8.30 What does Source 80 suggest about Yeats' attitude to the Rising?

The events of the next few years were to prove both Pearse and Yeats correct.

9

From Easter Rising to Partition 1916-1921

THE RISE OF SINN FÉIN

A number of events in the two and a half years following the Easter Rising completely changed the political situation in Ireland.

Redmond and Dillon, the Nationalist leaders in Parliament, had warned the government of the effect the executions of the rebel leaders could have.

"The wisest course is to execute no one for the present.... If there were shootings of prisoners on a large scale, the effect on public opinion might be disastrous in the extreme."

(John Dillon, in a letter to John Redmond, 30 April 1916.)

9.1 Why did Dillon believe that the effect of executions on public opinion could be "disastrous", when the attitude of the people towards the rebels was so hostile, as shown in Source 76?

The government ignored these warnings, and those rebel leaders who were executed became heroes, and a new generation of Irish martyrs was created to join those earlier martyrs such as Wolfe Tone, Robert Emmet and the Manchester Martyrs.

Having made the mistake of executing the leaders, the government made a further mistake by releasing the internees from their camp at Frongoch in north Wales in December 1916, and in June 1917 those who had been sentenced to imprisonment were also released. Many of these men were determined to continue the struggle, and one young survivor of the Easter Rising, **Michael Collins**, had already begun to build up the Irish Republican Brotherhood and to reorganize the Irish Volunteers, while in Frongoch.

The effect of the executions on public opinion was seen when four extreme nationalists, who were opposed to Home Rule, won by-elections during 1917. One of those elected was **Éamon de Valéra**, Commandant at Boland's Mill during the Easter Rising, who had been sentenced to death, but had been reprieved, partly due to the fact that he had been born in New York. The government had not wanted to anger the United States, whose support they hoped to gain for the war against Germany.

Meanwhile, attempts continued to find a peaceful solution which would enable Home Rule to come into effect after the War. An **Irish Convention** was held between July 1917 and April 1918, but Unionists and Nationalists failed to agree. This failure further weakened the position of Redmond's Nationalist Party.

During 1917, the government, which wrongly believed that Sinn Féin, the best known of the extremist groups, had organized the Easter Rising, continued to arrest leading members of Sinn Féin. One, **Thomas Ashe**, went on hunger strike, and he died in September 1917, after being fed by force. Michael Collins organized his funeral as a great demonstration, attended by 9000 Irish Volunteers and 30 000 other mourners, and at his graveside, Volunteers in uniform fired a volley of shots.

"Nothing additional remains to be said. The volley which we have just heard is the only speech which it is proper to make above the grave of a dead Fenian."

(Michael Collins, speaking at the funeral of Thomas Ashe, 25 September 1917.)

SOURCE 83

"The London *Daily Express* commented that Ashe's death made '100 000 Sinn Féiners out of 100 000 constitutional nationalists'."

(From R. Kee *Ireland: A History*, 1980.)

QUESTIONS

9.2 Of what event in 1915 does Source 82 remind you?

9.3 What do you think is meant by the *Daily Express* comment? Do you think it is true?

At a Sinn Féin Conference in October 1917, de Valéra produced a policy which united the various nationalist groups who were opposed to Home Rule. It set as its aim the establishment of an Irish Republic, and agreed not to send to Westminster any of their candidates who were elected to parliament. It therefore accepted the old Sinn Féin policy of boycotting all things British, but it did not rule out the use of force, as Arthur Griffith had always done. De Valéra was elected President of Sinn Féin, in place of Griffith, and Michael Collins became Director of Operations.

CONSCRIPTION

Sinn Féin's position was further strengthened by the government decision in April 1918 to extend conscription to Ireland. When it had been introduced in Great Britain in 1916, Ireland had been excluded, but the loss of 300 000 men during the Spring of 1918, meant that it was no longer enough to rely on men volunteering to serve in the army.

Again John Dillon, who had become leader of the Nationalist Party at Westminster following Redmond's death in March 1918, warned the government of the consequences. He said "All Ireland will rise against you," but the Bill was passed. The Nationalist M.P.s withdrew from Westminster, apparently accepting the Sinn Féin belief that nothing could be achieved by remaining there, and together with Sinn Féin, they organized a campaign against conscription, which included a general strike. The Roman Catholic Church also opposed conscription, and the Lord Mayor of Dublin called a conference, which agreed on a **National Pledge**, drawn up by de Valéra.

SOURCE 84

"Conscription ... [is a] law which the Irish have a right to resist by every means that are consonant [i.e. consistent] with the laws of God."

(Part of a statement made by the Irish Roman Catholic Bishops in April 1918.)

SOURCE 85

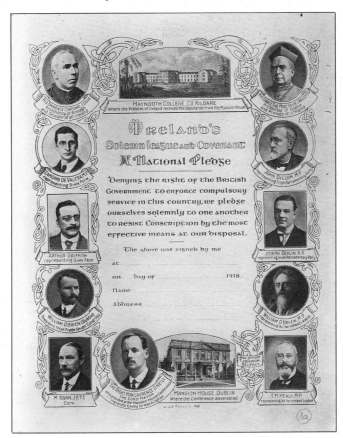

The National Pledge against conscription, which was signed by thousands in April 1918.

QUESTIONS

9.4 What evidence is there from Source 85 to support the idea shown in Source 84, that the Roman Catholic Church was opposed to conscription?

9.5 What evidence is there from Source 85 that both violent and non-violent nationalist politicians supported the National Pledge?

9.6 Is there any evidence in either Source 84 or Source 85 to suggest that violence might be used to resist conscription?

9.7 Where do you think de Valéra got the idea for a National Pledge? Give reasons for your answer.

The government claimed that Sinn Féin was involved in a German plot, and in May almost the entire leadership of the Irish Volunteers and Sinn Féin was arrested.

In the end, conscription was not extended to Ireland, and it was Sinn Féin which received the credit. The First World War ended in November 1918, and a month later a **General Election** was held, with an electorate three times larger than in 1910, because, for the first time, women and all men over 21 were allowed to vote.

SOURCE 86

"... Sinn Féin aims at securing the establishment of ... [the Irish] Republic.

1 By withdrawing the Irish representation from the British parliament and by denying the right and opposing the will of the British government or any other foreign government to legislate for Ireland.

2 By making use of any and every means available to render impotent [i.e. powerless] the power of England to hold Ireland in subjection by military force or otherwise.

3 By the establishment of a constituent assembly [i.e. parliament] ... as the supreme national authority to speak and act in the name of the Irish people....

4 By appealing to the Peace Conference for the establishment of Ireland as an independent nation ... on the principle of government by consent of the governed....

Sinn Féin ... stands by the Proclamation of the Provisional Government of Easter 1916....

The present Irish members of the English parliament constitute an obstacle to be removed.... By declaring their will to accept the status of a province instead of boldly taking their stand upon the right of the nation ... [and] by their persistent endeavours to induce the young manhood of Ireland to don the uniform of our seven-century oppressor, and place their lives at the disposal of the military machine that holds our nation in bondage, they endeavour to barter away ... the one great asset still left to our nation...."

(Extracts from the Sinn Féin *Manifesto to the Irish People*, 1918.)

SOURCE 87

Date	Liberal	Conservative/ Unionist	Labour	Irish Nationalist	Sinn Féin
1910	272	272	42	84	0
1918	161	383	73	7	73

(United Kingdom election results for 1910 and 1918.)

QUESTIONS

9.8 People often vote for a party on the basis of its manifesto. Do you think that the Sinn Féin Manifesto alone (Source 86) explains the support for Sinn Féin in the 1918 election? Read through this chapter again and make a list of other reasons which might help to explain Sinn Féin's success.

9.9 Find out what is meant by "the Peace Conference" in Source 86, point 4.

9.10 How does Source 86 help to explain the small number of Irish Nationalist M.P.s elected? Do you think that Source 86 is reliable evidence on which to base an answer to that question?

9.11 Is there any suggestion in Source 86 that violence might be used by Sinn Féin to achieve their aims?

DÁIL ÉIREANN AND THE I.R.A.

Several of the Sinn Féin candidates, including de Valéra, were elected for more than one seat. In fact only 69 Sinn Féiners were elected, including Countess Markievicz, the one woman who had been tried by court-martial after the Easter Rising, and the first woman to be elected to the House of Commons. Of those 69, 34 were in prison (including de Valéra and Griffith), one had been deported, two were ill, and 7 were absent on Sinn Féin business (including Collins, who was planning the successful escape of de Valéra from Lincoln Prison, which took place on 3 February 1919), and so only 25 were present when they held their first public meeting on 21 January 1919.

As they had promised, they did not go to Westminster, but instead they met in the Mansion House in Dublin and declared themselves to be "**Dáil Éireann**", the elected assembly of the Irish people.

SOURCE 88

"Whereas the Irish people is by right a free people:

And whereas for 700 years the Irish people has ... repeatedly protested in arms against foreign usurpation [i.e. take-over]:

And whereas English rule in this country is, and always has been, based on force ...:

And whereas the Irish Republic was proclaimed on Easter Monday 1916 by the Irish Republican Army, acting on behalf of the Irish people:

... And whereas ... the Irish electorate has in the general election of December 1918, seized the first occasion to declare by an overwhelming majority its firm allegiance to the Irish Republic:

Now therefore, we ... ratify [i.e. confirm] the establishment of the Irish Republic and pledge ourselves and our people to make this declaration effective by every means at our command.

... We solemnly declare foreign government in Ireland to be an invasion of our national right which we will never tolerate, and we demand the evacuation of our country by the English garrison:

... we humbly commit our destiny to Almighty God Who gave our fathers the courage and determination to persevere through long centuries of a ruthless tyranny, and ... we ask His Divine blessing on this the last stage of the struggle we have pledged ourselves to carry through to freedom."

(Extracts from the Irish Declaration of Independence in Dáil Éireann, 21 January 1919.)

9.12 What reasons are given for declaring the Irish Republic to be established?

9.13 What name is given to the rebels of Easter 1916? Explain what is meant by the name.

In April, after his return, de Valéra was appointed President, Griffith became Vice-President and among the ministers appointed was Michael Collins, Minister of Finance.

Most local councils outside the eastern part of Ulster recognized the authority of Dáil Éireann. Griffith established Sinn Féin law-courts; by 1921 almost 1000 were operating. Collins raised a loan of £350 000, and many paid their taxes to the Ministry of Finance. Sympathetic postal workers even diverted government mail to the Republican government departments.

THE ANGLO-IRISH WAR

However, British authority in Ireland could not have been undermined without military action, and the Irish Volunteers, now under a Chief of Staff, Richard Mulcahy, and renamed the **Irish Republican Army (I.R.A.)**, began to attack British forces in Ireland. The first incident took place at Soloheadbeg, County Tipperary, when a police convoy was ambushed. Guns and dynamite were captured and two constables in the Royal Irish Constabulary (R.I.C.) were killed.

"The principal means at the command of the Irish people is the Army of Ireland, and that army will be true to its trust.... If they are called on to shed blood in defence of the new-born Republic, they will not shrink from the sacrifice.

... Dáil Éireann ... declares a 'state of war' to exist between Ireland and England ...; it further declares that that state of war can never be ended until the English military invader evacuates our country....

The state of war ... justifies Irish Volunteers in treating the armed forces of the enemy—whether soldiers or policemen—exactly as a National Army would treat the members of an invading army....

Every Volunteer is entitled, morally and legally, ... to use all legitimate methods of warfare against the soldiers and policemen of the English usurper, and to slay them if necessary to do so in order to overcome their resistance...."

(An extract from *An t-Óglach*, the Irish Volunteers' newspaper, 31 January 1919.)

Q UESTIONS

9.14 Does Source 89 prove that all those who voted for Sinn Féin supported the use of violence?

9.15 Why does the writer say that a "state of war" existed? Do you think that the government would have seen it as a "state of war"? Give reasons for your answer.

9.16 What reasons are given for *not* regarding violence against the British forces as terrorism?

In September 1919, the government banned Dáil Éireann and Sinn Féin, and it imposed a curfew, but I.R.A. attacks continued, and hundreds of isolated police barracks had to be abandoned by the R.I.C., leaving large areas under I.R.A. control.

Not surprisingly, R.I.C. recruitment fell and there were many resignations, and so reinforcements were recruited in England. These men were mostly ex-soldiers, hardened by the violence of the First World War. Since there were not enough police uniforms, they were issued with a mixture of army and police uniforms, from which they gained the name "**the Black and Tans**". Officers known as "**Auxiliaries**" were also recruited.

Auxiliaries using a civilian hostage in the hope of preventing themselves from being attacked.

The government had perhaps 40 000 men operating in Ireland, against no more than 3000 I.R.A., but since the I.R.A. seldom wore uniforms, and since they often enjoyed support in the countryside, they were difficult to deal with.

The Black and Tans replied to I.R.A. ambushes with terror tactics. Village creameries were burnt down and houses in Balbriggan, Tuam and other towns were destroyed. In March 1920, Thomas MacCurtain, Lord Mayor of Cork, was shot dead by R.I.C. men in civilian clothes.

Although local units of the I.R.A. were given considerable freedom, Michael Collins acted as Director of Operations in Dublin. He organized a group, known as "**The Squad**", to kill informers and detectives, and he built up his own spy network. He often escaped capture only by minutes.

A photograph of a group of Black and Tans, which fell into the hands of the I.R.A. Several "Tans" have been marked out for assassination.

"In the summer of 1919 his [Collins'] sister ... came up by train ... to Dublin. It would be easy to identify her there, and only a matter of time before she led them to Collins. . . . The train reached Dublin at midnight. The platform was surrounded by military. The passengers were ordered to keep their seats. Word was passed that Michael Collins' sister was among them. . . . Michael saw her and pushed forward. He asked a porter the cause of the delay. The news that his own capture was imminent enraged him further. He stalked up to a British officer. That damned Collins again! This was his third hold-up that day on that blackguard's account. Here moreover was a lady who was ill. What possible use could there be in detaining her? The officer agreed that she certainly looked ill. . . . Michael courteously handed her out and ... escorted her from the station."

(An extract from M. Forester *Michael Collins: The Lost Leader*, published 1972.)

9.17 What can you learn about Michael Collins from Source 90?

9.18 Do you think that Source 90 gives you enough information to form an opinion about the kind of person Collins was?

In October 1920, Terence MacSwiney, the new Lord Mayor of Cork, who had been imprisoned for I.R.A. membership, died in Brixton Prison in London, after a 74-day hunger-strike. A week later, an 18-year-old student, Kevin Barry, was hanged in Dublin for his part in an I.R.A. ambush. Events such as these increased support for the I.R.A.

One of the worst exchanges of violence took place on Sunday 21 November 1920, which became known as "**Bloody Sunday**". That day the I.R.A. shot 11 government agents, 4 of them in their beds. Later that afternoon, the Black and Tans went to Croke Park, Dublin, where a Gaelic football match was being played. They fired into the crowd, killing 12 and injuring 60. That night, 3 of those who had been arrested were shot in Dublin Castle "while trying to escape", said the authorities.

For over two years dreadful acts were committed by both sides.

SOURCE 91

"The town of Balbriggan they've burned to the ground
While bullets like hailstones were whizzing around;
And women left homeless by this evil clan.
They've waged war on children, the bold Black and Tan.

From Dublin to Cork and from Thurles to Mayo
Lies a trail of destruction wherever they go;
With England to help and fierce passions to fan,
She must feel bloody proud of her bold Black and Tan.

Ah, then not by the terrors of England's foul horde,
For ne'er could a nation be ruled by the sword;
For our country we'll have yet in spite of her plan
Or ten times the number of bold Black and Tan.

We defeated conscription in spite of their threats,
And we're going to defeat old Lloyd George and his pets;
For Ireland and Freedom we're here to a man,
And we'll humble the pride of the bold Black and Tan."

(*The Bold Black and Tan*, a song popular in Ireland in 1920.)

SOURCE 92

"...two lorry loads of Auxiliaries ... were slowed down by a ruse [i.e. trick] and as the police climbed down from them they came under heavy fire; only one man survived.... The very next day another ambush only a few miles from Cork City caused more Auxiliary casualties and that night Auxiliaries and Black and Tans poured into the town, looting, wrecking, drinking and burning—burning to such effect, indeed, that a large part of the centre of the city was completely destroyed, while the fire brigade was deliberately obstructed as they sought to bring the flames under control.... The Auxiliaries made their own comment on the affair when they swaggered about the streets of Dublin with burnt corks in their caps."

(An extract from F. S. L. Lyons *Ireland Since the Famine*, published in 1973.)

A photograph of part of Cork city centre after the Black and Tan attack in December 1920.

QUESTIONS

9.19 Is there any evidence that Source 91 is biased?

9.20 "Biased evidence is of no value to the historian." Do you agree? Give reasons for your answer.

9.21 What evidence is there from Source 91 to suggest that the Black and Tan tactics would not be successful?

9.22 In what ways do Source 92 and Source 93 support Source 91? Do they make Source 91 any more reliable?

THE GOVERNMENT OF IRELAND ACT, 1920

The extent of the violence in Ireland led to demands in Britain for an attempt to find a peaceful solution.

It was recognized that the Ulster Unionists could not be forced to accept a Home Rule parliament in Dublin, now that nationalist opinion had become so extreme, and so David Lloyd George, who had succeeded Asquith as Prime Minister in 1916, introduced a new Bill "For the Better Government of Ireland", which was passed in December 1920.

This **Government of Ireland Act** accepted the idea that Ireland should be divided or partitioned—something to which both Unionists and Nationalists had been opposed in the past. The Act created the state of **Northern Ireland**, which was to consist of the 6 counties in the north-east of Ulster,

(Antrim, Armagh, Down, Fermanagh, Londonderry and Tyrone), with a parliament in Belfast. A separate parliament was to be set up in Dublin for the remaining 26 counties. The powers granted to these parliaments were similar to those granted under the Third Home Rule Bill of 1912. In the hope that Ireland would eventually be reunited, a **Council of Ireland** was to be set up, to consider matters which concerned both parts of Ireland. Its members were to be elected from within the two Irish parliaments. "On the date of the Irish union" the Council of Ireland was to cease to exist. "**Partition**" was clearly not seen as a permanent situation.

SOURCE 94

THE KINDEST CUT OF ALL.

WELSH WIZARD. "I NOW PROCEED TO CUT THIS MAP INTO TWO PARTS AND PLACE THEM IN THE HAT. AFTER A SUITABLE INTERVAL THEY WILL BE FOUND TO HAVE COME TOGETHER OF THEIR OWN ACCORD—(ASIDE)—AT LEAST LET'S HOPE SO; I'VE NEVER DONE THIS TRICK BEFORE."

A cartoonist's view of the Government of Ireland Act.

 UESTIONS

9.23 Why do you think it was decided to set up two parliaments in Ireland?

9.24 What is the attitude of the cartoonist to the Government of Ireland Act? Does he expect it to be a success? Do you think he was just expressing a personal opinion, or might he be voicing the feeling of others?

9.25 How would you expect the Act to be viewed by:

(a) Unionists?

(b) Nationalists?

(c) Sinn Féiners?

Give reasons for your answers.

The Ulster Unionists accepted the parliament in Belfast, although they did not like deserting the Unionists in the south.

SOURCE 95

"It has been said that this Bill lends itself to the union of Ulster and the rest of Ireland. It would not be fair to the House if I lent the slightest hope of the union arising within the lifetime of any man in this House. I do not believe it for a moment ... because [the Bill] gives Ulster a parliament of its own, and sets up a state of affairs which will prevent, I believe, for all time Ulster being forced into a parliament in Dublin without its own consent; because it does those two things, I say that the Bill practically gives us everything that we fought for, everything that we armed ourselves for and for which we raised our [Ulster] Volunteers."

(Sir James Craig speaking in the House of Commons during the debate on the Government of Ireland Bill, 29 March 1920.)

SOURCE 96

"Sir Edward Carson and the Ulster Unionists did not like it; partition was not what they were after, and especially a partition which gave them only six of Ulster's nine counties.

With the cold logic that ran through his bigotry, however, Carson accepted the loss of Donegal, Cavan and Monaghan as a matter of inevitable mathematics. By leaving out the Protestants of those three counties, he avoided bringing into the Northern Province an additional 260 000 Roman Catholics."

(An extract from D. Norman *Terrible Beauty: A Life of Constance Markievicz*, published in 1987.)

QUESTIONS

9.26 Does James Craig believe that the Wizard's "trick" (Source 94) will work? What reasons does he give for his belief?

9.27 Compare the last sentence of Source 95 with the first sentence of Source 96. In what way do they disagree? Is either source more reliable than the other? Explain your answer.

9.28 Why had the Unionists armed themselves and set up the U.V.F. in 1913? Did the 1920 Government of Ireland Act give them "everything that we fought for"? If not, why do you think Craig supported it?

9.29 According to Source 96, why did the Unionists not ask for all 9 Ulster counties to be included in Northern Ireland?

In May 1921, elections were held for the two new parliaments in Ireland. In Northern Ireland, the Unionists won 40 out of the 52 seats, and on 22 June 1921, King George V formally opened the Parliament of Northern Ireland in Belfast. **James Craig**, who had been leader of the Unionists since Carson's resignation earlier that year, became the first **Prime Minister of Northern Ireland**, although the I.R.A. refused to recognize the authority of the new government and so violence continued. That situation, and rumours of ill-treatment of Protestants in the south, stirred up sectarian hatred in Northern Ireland and during the summer of 1920, there were attacks on Catholic areas, resulting in 62 deaths. The birth of Northern Ireland was marked by bloodshed.

10 The Treaty and the Civil War 1921-1923

In the south, the Government of Ireland Act was virtually ignored. In the elections of May 1921, 124 Sinn Féin candidates were elected unopposed, and they took their seats in Dáil Éireann. Only the four Unionists, elected to represent Trinity College, Dublin, attended the first meeting of the southern parliament.

The Anglo-Irish War continued, but both sides felt that it had reached a military stalemate. In July 1921, a truce was agreed. During the course of the war, over 1300 people had been killed.

The fighting had stopped, but a final peace settlement was not easy to find. Sinn Féin wanted a totally independent republic, which included the whole of Ireland; the British government would only agree to limited independence, within the British Empire, and it would not force the Ulster Unionists to accept government from Dublin.

In October 1921, Arthur Griffith, Michael Collins and other Irish delegates went to London to meet a British delegation which included David Lloyd George and Winston Churchill. The negotiations dragged on for weeks and then, in December, Lloyd George made his final offer.

THE ANGLO-IRISH TREATY 1921

Ireland was to be called "**The Irish Free State**" and it was to be self-governing, with a parliament, free to make laws, but it was to remain part of the British Empire—a British Dominion—with the same degree of independence as the Dominion of Canada.

Members of the Irish parliament would have to swear loyalty to the King, who would be represented in Ireland by a Governor-General. The British agreed to remove their army from Ireland, but Britain was to have the right to use naval bases at Cobh, Berehaven and Lough Swilly.

The Northern Ireland Parliament could ask that the 6 counties of Northern Ireland should be excluded, and, if it did, then Northern Ireland was to remain part of the United Kingdom, and not part of the Irish Free State. A Boundary Commission was to be set up to decide on the exact border between Northern Ireland and the Free State, and Lloyd George convinced Collins that the Commission would give at least 2 of the 6 counties of Northern Ireland to the Free State, and that the remaining part of Northern Ireland would be too small to survive. (In fact, when it did report in 1925, the Commission proposed such minor changes, that the border was left exactly as it was.)

On 5 December, Lloyd George told the Irish delegation that they must sign, or renew the war. They knew that a renewal of the war would be unpopular in Ireland, and so, on 6 December 1921, they signed the "**Articles of Agreement for a Treaty**".

months from the date hereof.

18. This instrument shall be submitted forthwith by His Majesty's Government forthe approval of Parliament, and by the Irish signatories to a meeting summoned for the purpose of the members elected to sit in the House of Commons of Southern Ireland, and if approved shall be ratified by the necessary legislation.

The last page of the "Articles of Agreement for a Treaty", with the signatures of the Irish delegates in Irish, and the signatures of the British delegates. The document could not be called a "Treaty" until it had been approved by both the United Kingdom Parliament and Dáil Éireann.

SOURCE 97

"Think—what have I got for Ireland? Something which she has wanted for these past 700 years. Will anyone be satisfied at the bargain? Will anyone? I tell you this—early this morning I signed my death warrant. I thought at the time, how odd, how ridiculous—a bullet may just as well have done the job five years ago."

(From a letter written by Michael Collins to a friend on the day the Treaty was signed.)

QUESTIONS

10.1 From what Collins said in Source 97, do you think he was satisfied with the Treaty he had signed? If not, why do you think he signed it?

10.2 What parts of the Treaty do you think that Collins, Griffith and the other Irish delegates were most unhappy about?

10.3 What do you think Collins meant when he said "I signed my death warrant"?

10.4 What is the significance of "five years ago"?

Although many in Ireland were pleased that the war was over, de Valéra was angry that the delegates had signed the Treaty without consulting him, and that they had settled for less than the Irish Republic, for which they had been fighting. Some extreme republicans called for a renewal of the war. Others argued that the Treaty was the best they could have got, and that it was far more than they could have hoped for ten years earlier.

SOURCE 98

(A) "... I am against this treaty because it does not reconcile [i.e. agree with] Irish national aspirations [i.e. hopes] with association with the British government. I am against this treaty not because I am a man of war, but a man of peace. I am against this treaty because it will not end the centuries of conflict between the two nations of Great Britain and Ireland.... I would rather see the same thing over again than that Irishmen should have to hang their heads in shame for having signed ... a document handing over their authority to a foreign country.... Does this assembly think the Irish people have changed so much within the past year or two that they now want to get into the British empire after seven centuries of fighting? ..."

(Éamon de Valéra speaking in the Dáil on 19 December 1921, during the debate on the Treaty.)

(B) "... We were sent to make some compromise, bargain or arrangement; we made an arrangement; the arrangement we made is not satisfactory to many people.... That treaty is not an ideal thing; it has its faults.... But ... we have a treaty signed by the heads of the British government; ... I could draw up a much better treaty myself, one that would suit myself; but it is not going to be passed [by the British]. We are, therefore, face to face with a practical situation.... We here can accept the treaty, and deal with it in good faith with the English people, and ... reach, if we desire it, any further status that we desire or require after. Who is going to say what the world is to be like in ten years hence? We can make peace on the basis of that treaty; it does not for ever bind us not to ask for any more.... This treaty gives the Irish people what they have not had for centuries; it gives them a foothold in their own country; it gives them solid ground on which to stand; ...."

(Arthur Griffith speaking in the Dáil on 7 January 1922, during the debate on the Treaty.)

10.5 What objections did de Valéra have to the Treaty (Source 98A)?

10.6 Was Griffith perfectly satisfied with the Treaty (Source 98B)?

10.7 What reasons did he give for accepting the Treaty, even though it was not perfect (Source 98B)?

10.8 Which of the two do you think had the stronger argument? Give reasons for your answer.

10.9 Do you think (a) Redmond, and (b) Pearse (both of whom were dead), would have approved of the Treaty? Give reasons for your answer.

10.10 What would you expect the attitude of the Ulster Unionists to the Treaty to have been?

(A) "Take it down from the mast, Irish traitors,
'Tis the flag we Republicans claim.
It can never be owned by Free Staters
Who shed on it nothing but shame.
Then leave it to those who are willing
To uphold it in war or in peace,
Those men who intend to do killing
Until England's tyranny cease."

(An extract from a song *Soldiers of '22*.)

(B) "I went to see David, to London to David,
I went to see David and what did he do?
He gave me a Free State, a nice little Free State,
A Free State that's tied up in Red, White and Blue.

I brought it to Dublin to show to Dáil Éireann.
I brought it to Dublin and what did they do?
They asked me what kind of a thing was a Free State,
A Free State that's tied up in Red, White and Blue.

Three-quarters of Ireland a nation—I told them,
Tied on to the Empire with Red, White and Blue;
And an oath they must swear to King George and Queen Mary,
An oath they must swear to the son-in-law new.*

I'm teaching them Irish and painting their boxes
All over with green, sure what more can I do?
Yet they tell me they want just an Irish Republic
Without any trimmings of Red, White and Blue."

(An extract from a poem *The Irish Free State.*)
*The reference to "the son-in-law new" must apply to the Earl of Harewood,
who married The Princess Royal, daughter of George V, on 28 February 1922.

Q UESTIONS

10.11 In what way does Source 99A suggest that the fears expressed by Collins in Source 97 might have been well founded?
10.12 What objections does the writer of Source 99B have to the Treaty?
10.13 According to Source 99B, what changes were being made in Ireland to make the country more "Irish"?
10.14 What is the value of Sources 99A and 99B to the historian?

When the vote was taken in the Dáil on 7 January 1922, the Treaty was accepted by 64 votes to 57. Those who voted against it included de Valéra, Patrick Pearse's mother, Thomas Clarke's widow and Terence MacSwiney's sister.

De Valéra resigned and was replaced by Griffith as President of Dáil Éireann, while Collins became Chairman of the Provisional Government which was to conduct the business of taking over from the British authorities.

The British army began to withdraw from the Free State, and it handed over its barracks to the local I.R.A. units—in some cases supporters of the Treaty and in some cases opponents of it.

In March 1922, some of the anti-Treaty I.R.A., led by Rory O'Connor, occupied the Four Courts and other places in Dublin.

A general election was held in the Free State in June 1922. One of the main issues was the Treaty.

SOURCE 100

Think, People, Think

Do YOU thoroughly UNDERSTAND the issue?

Are you, by your Free Vote, going to disestablish the Republic of Ireland for which many brave young men have DIED, and for which Thousands of our Countrymen have risked all, to uphold,

REMEMBER—this will be the Immediate Result

of the Establishment of a Free State Government

The glorious achievements of our "Flying Columns" under most trying circumstances, and against such fearful odds, can find no parallel in the World's history; nor can any future generation of TRUE Irishmen fail to remember or glory in the deeds of such Heroes. Some have nobly perished, but—

What did they FIGHT AND DIE FOR?

Was it that Ireland, by foregoing her claim as a Sovereign State, should accept as a Final Settlement a status less than that of a British Dominion, and thereby strengthen the position of the British Empire to our own detriment?

UNDOUBTEDLY NO! and the person who states that these men laboured for any other purpose but the upholding of the IRISH REPUBLIC, established in 1916, is but trying to belie his own conscience.

Will YOU be a party to lowering the Flag of the

Republic, stained only by the Blood of Irish Martyrs?

By recording your Vote for the Free State, you are, perhaps unconsciously, doing your utmost to tighten the bonds of slavery on our Country, and future generations shall curse those responsible for surrendering our position at a most unique moment. Remember, there will not, and cannot, be peace in Ireland until the might of the British Empire has vanished in every form from our sight.

A COLLECTION will be made throughout the Constituency of South Cork for the purpose of defraying Expenses in connection with the General Election.

Rally to the Standard of the Republic!

Long Live the Republic!

An election poster in June 1922, explaining the reasons for voting for de Valéra and those who opposed the Treaty.

QUESTIONS

10.15 Pick out four phrases which show that Source 100 contains bias. Explain in what way your chosen phrases are biased.

10.16 Which sentence in Source 100 helps to explain the continuation of I.R.A. violence into the 1980s?

CIVIL WAR 1922–1923

The result of the election was that 35 out of the 128 T.D.s (members of the Dáil) opposed the Treaty. Those election results, along with the kidnapping of a Free State General by O'Connor's men, and the murder in London of Field Marshal Sir Henry Wilson, M.P. for North Down and security adviser to the Northern Ireland government, persuaded Collins to take action, and on 27 June 1922, the Free State army attacked the Four Courts. This marked the beginning of a civil war between former comrades—the Free State Army and the so-called "**Irregular**" **I.R.A.**—all of whom had been fighting together against the British only a year before. Collins found that, for once, he had something in common with Sir James Craig.

SOURCE 101

THE MAD BULL.

FARMER CRAIG. "IF YOU CAN'T KEEP THAT BRUTE ON YOUR SIDE OF THE FENCE I SHALL DEAL WITH HIM AS I THINK FIT."

FARMER COLLINS. "WELL, BETWEEN YOU AND ME, I WISH TO GOD YE WOULD."

A British cartoon, published in 1922.

10.17 What "brute" is "Farmer Craig" referring to in Source 101?

10.18 What is represented by "the fence"?

10.19 The majority of the people in the north accepted the Government of Ireland Act, and the majority of the people in the south accepted the Treaty. How does Source 101 help to explain why violence in Ireland continued?

A photograph showing the damage done to the Four Courts building during the Civil War. Many valuable historical records were destroyed.

"Irregular" I.R.A. on the streets of Dublin during the Civil War.

The Civil War in the Free State lasted for almost a year and cost perhaps 4000 lives. The Free State government had been forced to intern without trial 11 000 Republicans, and to execute 77—even more than the British had done during the Anglo-Irish War.

Two men who did not live to see the end of the Civil War were Arthur Griffith, who died of a brain haemorrhage in August 1922, and Michael Collins, who was killed in a Republican ambush ten days later.

Richard Mulcahy, Minister of Defence and Chief of Staff of the Army of the Irish Free State, and formerly Chief of Staff of the I.R.A., with Michael Collins, Minister of Finance and Commander in Chief of the Free State Army, at the funeral of Arthur Griffith in August 1922, only a week before Collins' death in a Republican ambush in his home county of Cork.

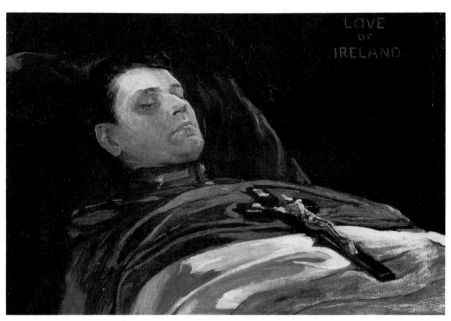

Michael Collins' prophecy fulfilled. A painting of the dead Michael Collins by Sir John Lavery.

In May 1923 de Valéra recognized that his "Irregulars" were heavily outnumbered and that continued resistance was pointless. He ordered his supporters to lay down their arms, although, despite the end of the Civil War, the Republic lived on in the minds of many of them.

The new President, **William Cosgrave**, now had to attempt the difficult task of healing the divisions and of bringing peace and prosperity to the Irish Free State.

Conclusion:
Ireland since the Treaty

Much has happened in Ireland since 1923; so much, in fact, that it would require another book to deal with it. But has anything changed?

In 1932 de Valéra's new political party, **Fianna Fáil**, won the general election in the Free State. His government almost immediately took advantage of the Statute of Westminster of 1931, by which British Dominions were free to repeal Acts of the United Kingdom Parliament. In 1933 the Oath of Allegiance taken by T.D.s was abolished, and in 1937 a new Constitution was drawn up. It abolished the office of Governor-General and replaced the name "Irish Free State" with the name "**Éire**" (Ireland). Article 2 of the new Constitution included the words "... the national territory consists of the whole island of Ireland ...", and Article 41.1 recognized "the special position" of the Roman Catholic Church. Both those statements helped to confirm the fears of the Unionists in Northern Ireland.

In 1948 Dáil Éireann passed The Republic of Ireland Act, which cut the remaining connections with Britain and gave Éire the name "**Republic of Ireland**", with effect from Easter Monday 1949.

The United Kingdom Parliament replied with the Ireland Act (1949), which recognized that the Republic of Ireland had "ceased ... to be part of His Majesty's Dominions", and then went on to state that Northern Ireland could not "cease to be part of ... the United Kingdom without the consent of the Parliament of Northern Ireland".

In Northern Ireland, the Unionists, who made up the majority of the population, controlled the government of Northern Ireland for over 50 years. The treatment of the nationalist minority in Northern Ireland during that 50 years provoked unrest in the late 1960s, and a renewal of I.R.A. activity, with which the Northern Ireland government proved incapable of dealing, led to the suspension of the parliament of Northern Ireland and to the imposition of direct rule from Westminster in 1972.

To this day, members of the I.R.A. look back to 1916, when Patrick Pearse had declared all of Ireland to be an independent Republic, while to Ulster Unionists, the reasons which led them to oppose Home Rule a hundred years ago, still seem valid. They still view Dublin interference in the affairs of Northern Ireland with hostility and many of them even oppose the co-operation between the United Kingdom government and the government of the Irish Republic against the I.R.A.

The **Anglo-Irish Agreement** signed by the Prime Ministers of the United Kingdom and the Irish Republic in 1985, which aimed "to reconcile the two major traditions in Ireland" (Nationalist and Unionist), has not yet achieved its aim.

"**The Irish Question**" seems no nearer to being answered.

THE VIOLENT REPUBLICAN TRADITION

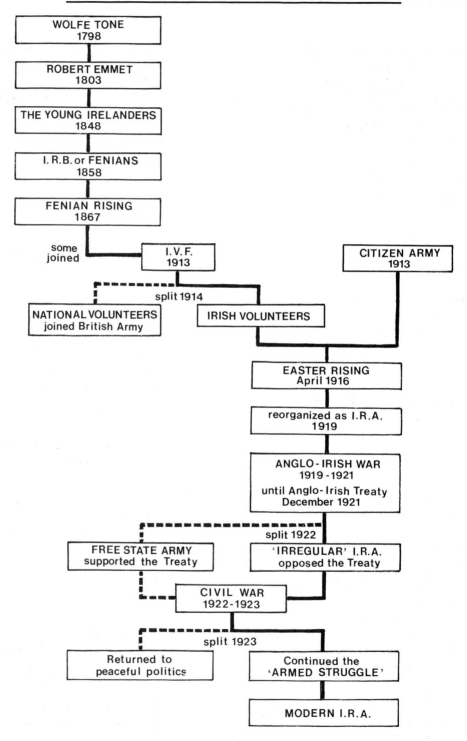

WOLFE TONE
1798

ROBERT EMMET
1803

THE YOUNG IRELANDERS
1848

I. R. B. or FENIANS
1858

FENIAN RISING
1867

some joined

I.V.F.
1913

CITIZEN ARMY
1913

split 1914

NATIONAL VOLUNTEERS
joined British Army

IRISH VOLUNTEERS

EASTER RISING
April 1916

reorganized as I.R.A.
1919

ANGLO-IRISH WAR
1919-1921

until Anglo-Irish Treaty
December 1921

split 1922

FREE STATE ARMY
supported the Treaty

'IRREGULAR' I.R.A.
opposed the Treaty

CIVIL WAR
1922-1923

split 1923

Returned to
peaceful politics

Continued the
'ARMED STRUGGLE'

MODERN I.R.A.

Index